Eight Philosophers
of the
Italian Renaissance

Eight Philosophers
of the
Italian Renaissance

Paul Oskar Kristeller

STANFORD UNIVERSITY PRESS
STANFORD CALIFORNIA

To John H. Randall, Jr.
in friendship and gratitude

Preface

This little volume is based on the Arensberg Lectures given at Stanford University under the auspices of the Francis Bacon Foundation in May 1961. The purpose of the lectures was to give a brief survey of Italian thought during the Renaissance period, and they cover at least in part the same subject that I have treated many times during the last twenty years or so in a graduate lecture course at Columbia University. The entire subject of Renaissance philosophy is obviously too large for adequate treatment in a course, let alone in a series of lectures. A small selection had to be made, which was bound to be arbitrary and determined by the limitations of my knowledge and interests. In mitigation of these shortcomings, I can only say that the thinkers selected are to some extent representative, and that the information given about them is as accurate as I could make it. My colleagues at Stanford University must share the responsibility for this volume, since it was their friendly insistence that prompted me to deliver and publish these lectures. However, I may say in defense of my effort what has been said about a number of bad books, that it offers the only treatment of a worthwhile subject that is available in English in a single volume.

A ninth lecture, which was not a part of the series but delivered on a different occasion, has been added as an appendix. It is quite general in content and might have been used as an introductory chapter. However, since it overlaps with the main series, and since it concerns only humanism, not the whole of Renaissance thought, I have preferred to use it as an appendix. This lecture, which I gave at Cornell University, at the Dumbarton Oaks Research Library, and at the University of Illinois, as well as at Stanford, is closely related to some papers I have already published, and hence it has received no annotation in this volume.

In preparing the lectures for publication, I have thoroughly revised their style, but have left their general content pretty much intact. In accordance with valuable suggestions received from the Stanford Press and its readers, I have added some footnotes and a bibliography. I obviously could not attempt to give a complete documentation for a book of this nature, but I have tried to indicate at least some of the sources on which my account is based, and I should like to encourage the reader, especially the student, to do some further reading on the subject. In citing passages from the authors discussed, I have given in most instances my own translations, but indicated in the footnotes both the original text editions and the English translations that are the most readily obtainable. In a few instances, I have cited the original Latin or Italian text in the notes, since I consider translations merely an imperfect substitute, and always wish to emphasize the need for grasping the nuances and the terminology and wording of an original text. The method of annotation varies from chapter to chapter. In citing authors who treat their subject in a clear and coherent fashion, such as Telesio and Patrizi, I have often simply given chapter references in the text itself instead of supplying precise references in footnotes. For authors whose ideas are scattered rather than systematically developed, precise references to specific paragraphs or sentences were necessary. In the case of Ficino, I ventured to refer to my book on him, in which his ideas are discussed and documented more fully than would have been possible in this volume. My explicit references to Bruno are limited to his chief Italian dialogues.

I have tended to avoid polemics in this volume, although many of my remarks are critical of the views of other scholars, at least by implication. I should perhaps apologize for the numerous obiter dicta, which helped to enliven the lectures when delivered and which I was encouraged to retain in the published version.

I should like to thank my colleagues at Stanford University for their friendly interest and hospitality, especially Professors John Goheen, Richard Jones, John Mothershead, Lawrence Ryan, Patrick Suppes, and Virgil Whitaker, and to express my appreciation to the Stanford University Press, and especially to Mr. J. G. Bell and Miss Pauline Wickham, for their suggestions and interest. I am indebted to Professors Charles B. Schmitt and Charles Trinkaus for several important references, and to Professor John H. Randall, Jr., of Columbia University and Mr. W. H. Bond of the Harvard University Library for having made available to me, at a crucial moment, some books that were indispensable for the completion of the volume.

P. O. K.

New York, Columbia University
January 4, 1964

Contents

Eight Philosophers

of the

Italian Renaissance

Petrarch

In 1960 exactly a hundred years had passed since Jacob Burckhardt published his famous essay *The Civilization of the Renaissance in Italy*, and in a sense we were celebrating at that time the centenary of Renaissance studies. If we look back upon the development of the field during this period, we notice a confusing variety of opinions and interpretations, and at the same time an impressive accumulation of new facts and new perspectives that is still far from being completed. Thus the picture drawn by Burckhardt has undergone considerable change, yet his book has not been replaced by an equally comprehensive synthesis, and many scholars will now agree that there remains a valid core in Burckhardt's views, although they are obviously in need of being corrected and supplemented in many ways.

One of the numerous questions Burckhardt's work has left to his successors concerns the position of Italy within the period that we should like to extend roughly from the early fourteenth century to the end of the sixteenth. Whereas Burckhardt had limited his study to Italy, historians interested in the contributions of other European countries during the same period were called upon to decide to what extent these contributions were due to native developments or to Italian influences. For Burckhardt's basic claim that Italy during the period with which we are concerned occupied a place of unique importance can hardly be questioned, and it is this fact, as well as the limitations of my knowledge, that may justify my decision to restrict these lectures to a series of Italian thinkers—although it would be easy to find a number of Renaissance thinkers from other countries who might have an equal claim on our attention.

Within the broader area of Renaissance studies, the philosophical thought of the period has remained a comparatively neglected field. General students of the period, including Burckhardt himself, have tended to pay less attention to its philosophy than to its political and religious history, or to its contributions in literature and the arts, the sciences and classical learning. Philosophers, on the other hand, in dealing with the history of their subject, have traditionally focused on ancient and modern philosophy, and have but recently begun to turn their attention to medieval thought. The large amount of work dedicated to Renaissance thought by Fiorentino and Dilthey, Cassirer and Gentile, Garin, Nardi, and many other scholars has not yet been sufficiently absorbed by the average textbook or course on the history of philosophy; and, furthermore, these scholars themselves are far from having exhausted the subject.

The reasons for this state of affairs are not too difficult to see. The philosophical literature of the Renaissance does not offer any great names of unquestioned eminence such as Plato or Aristotle, Thomas Aquinas or Descartes. Moreover, the meaning of philosophy, and its relations to the other branches of knowledge, have been subject to a good deal of historical change, and if we construe the content and task of philosophy exclusively in terms of some modern school of thought, whether pragmatism or analytical philosophy, existentialism or Neo-Thomism, large areas of past thought that might otherwise form a significant part of the history of philosophy become irrelevant. A historian of culture, on the other hand, who tries to understand the stylistic unity of a period in all its manifestations, may easily become impatient with the professional philosophers of the period he is trying to understand, because their use of a certain terminology, and their concern with certain technical problems, seem to link them more closely with their fellow philosophers of other periods than with the climate of opinion of their own time.

In spite of these difficulties, I am inclined to believe that the study of Renaissance philosophy will be of continuing, and even increasing, interest both to the student of the Renaissance and to the student of philosophy and its history. For the philosophical thought of the Renaissance provides important analogies and sources for an understanding of the arts and literature, religion and sciences of the period, and it helps the historian of philosophy to understand the difference in outlook that separates, say, Bacon and Descartes from Aquinas or Ockham. In trying to discuss a few of the more significant thinkers of the period, I shall cover but a very small sector of a broad and highly complex area that includes a good deal of additional and partly uncharted territory.

The earliest and most pervasive intellectual movement that affected the history of philosophical thought during the period is Renaissance humanism. The meaning of this movement has been subject to many debates and misunderstandings in recent years. If we want to reach a proper understanding of it, we must first of all try to forget the rather vague overtones of an emphasis on human values that the term humanism has acquired in present-day language. Moreover, in order to grasp the meaning of humanism for the Renaissance, I have found it helpful to go back from the term humanism, which was coined in the early nineteenth century, to the terms humanist and humanities, from which it was derived, and which were actually used during the Renaissance. It appears clear from the sources of the period that a humanist was a teacher of the humanities, or *studia humanitatis*, and that the term humanities stood for a cycle of disciplines comprising grammar, rhetoric, poetry, history, and moral philosophy.

It will be apparent from this definition that Renaissance humanism consisted in a great rise and development of the humanities thus understood, and that any influence it may have had on other areas of civiliza-

3

tion such as the arts and literature, the sciences and religion, must have been of an indirect nature.

Moreover, I do not think that it is possible to define Renaissance humanism by a set of specific philosophical ideas shared by all humanists, or to regard humanism exclusively as a philosophical movement, let alone as the sum total of Renaissance philosophy as some scholars have recently tended to do. A very large part of the work of the humanists was scholarly or literary rather than philosophical, even in the broadest possible sense of the word, and many humanists who were distinguished scholars or writers made no significant contribution even to that branch of philosophy, ethics, which was considered a part of their province. On the other hand, comparatively few humanists made a direct contribution to those philosophical disciplines that lay outside their own province, such as logic, metaphysics, or natural philosophy, and the thinkers who carried on the main work in these fields, though often imbued with a humanist, that is, classical and literary training, cannot be simply classified or labeled as humanists. Finally, if we compare the work of different humanists, we are led to the conclusion that they held a great variety of opinions and ideas, and that their common denominator is to be found in an educational, scholarly, and stylistic ideal, and in the range of their problems and interests, rather than in their allegiance to any given set of philosophical or theological views.

In other words, if we want to do justice to the Renaissance humanists, we should realize that they were scholars and writers as well as thinkers, and that their contribution to philosophy, which must be our main concern as historians of philosophy, was supplemented and colored by those other, non-philosophical preoccupations. To my mind there is nothing wrong about a philosopher being engaged at the same time in other intellectual pursuits. Yet somehow we are more accustomed to the philosopher who is also a theologian or a scientist, and must be reminded that there have been philosophers whose additional interests and pursuits were scholarly and literary rather than theological or scientific, and this was precisely the case of the Renaissance humanists.

Hence we may appreciate, too, the powerful indirect influence Renaissance humanism had upon the history of philosophy, apart from the specific ideas it contributed to it. If modern philosophers have been writing essays and lectures, papers and treatises, rather than questions and commentaries, they are unwittingly carrying on a tradition that in modern times began with Renaissance humanism. And if they have been able to read not only Aristotle in translation and Thomas Aquinas, but also Aristotle in the original as well as Plato and many other Greek philosophers either in the original or in translation, they are indebted for this enrichment of their philosophical library to the work done by the Renaissance humanists.

The author with whom we are beginning our survey of a few selected Renaissance thinkers, Petrarch, has often been called the initiator of Renaissance humanism, but I should prefer to call him its first great representative, and he was probably the earliest humanist who had a significant impact upon the thought of his time. Francesco Petrarca was born in Arezzo in 1304 into an exiled Florentine family, and taken to Avignon at the age of 8. After studying law at Montpellier and Bologna, he spent the period from 1326 to 1353 in Avignon, which was then the seat of the papal Curia. During this time he made several long journeys to Italy. In 1353, he moved to Italy and spent the rest of his life in his native country, mainly in Milan, Venice, and Padua. He died in Arquà, near Padua, in 1374. He held several ecclesiastical benefices, and also enjoyed the patronage of the Colonna and the Visconti, whom he seems to have served on occasion as a secretary.

In modern times, Petrarch has owed his fame mainly to his Italian poems, which have secured him an outstanding place in the history of literature. Yet for Petrarch himself and for his contemporaries, as well as for several subsequent generations down to the sixteenth century, his numerous Latin writings were as important as his Italian verse. These Latin writings show a great variety in form and content, and are in a sense representative of humanist literature. They include Latin poems, orations and invectives, a few historical works, and a large body of letters which were preserved, collected, and edited by the author as carefully as his other literary compositions.

A last group of his works belongs to the field of moral philosophy, and is therefore of more immediate interest for our purpose. It includes such writings as the dialogue "On the Remedies of Good and Bad Fortune" (*De remediis utriusque fortunae*, 1366), and the treatises "On the Secret Conflict of My Worries" (*De secreto conflictu curarum mearum*, better known as *Secretum*, completed before 1358), "On the Solitary Life" (*De vita solitaria*, 1356), and "On His Own and Many Other People's Ignorance" (*De sui ipsius et multorum ignorantia*, 1367).

It is mainly in these writings and in his letters, unmethodical and loosely composed in their reasoning as they are, that we have to look for Petrarch's philosophical opinions. Much of his thought consists of tendencies and aspirations rather than of developed ideas or doctrines, and it is inextricably linked with his learning and reading, his tastes and feelings. Nevertheless it is significant, both for his own sake and for the tremendous influence it was to exercise on several generations of humanists. Since Petrarch's ideas are never stated in a systematic fashion, we must try to reconstruct them from a number of scattered remarks.

An important aspect of Petrarch's thought, one that was to be developed by many later humanists down to Vives, was his hostility toward scholasticism, that is, the university learning of the later Middle Ages. He attacked astrology as well as logic and jurisprudence, and dedicated entire works to criticizing the physicians and the Aristotelian philosophers. Yet these attacks, sweeping and suggestive as they are, do not enter very far into the specific problems or methods of the disciplines attacked; they are highly personal and subjective, and they reflect personal conflicts and rivalries between Petrarch and some representatives of these other fields, rather than differences of opinion on specific issues or arguments. When Petrarch rejects the authority of Aristotle or of his Arabic commentator Averroes, he does so from personal dislike rather than on objective grounds; and when he criticizes such theories as the eternity of the world, the attainment of perfect happiness during the present life, or the so-called theory of the double truth (that is, of the separate validity of Aristotelian philosophy and of Christian theology, a theory held by many Aristotelian philosophers of the time), his main argument is that these doctrines are contrary to the Christian religion.

Yet the positive value that Petrarch opposed to medieval science was neither a new science nor merely religious faith, but the study of classical antiquity, a pursuit in which he had engaged with great enthusiasm since his early years. All his life, Petrarch was an avid and attentive reader of the ancient Latin writers: he copied, collected, and annotated their works, and tried to correct their texts, and to appropriate their style and ideas. When he came upon Cicero's letters to Atticus in Verona, he rediscovered these classical texts, which had been almost unknown during the preceding centuries, thus initiating a series of similar discoveries for which Poggio and other later humanists were to become famous. The reading of the ancient Latin writers, and the sight of Rome's ancient monuments, evoked in Petrarch as in many other Italian humanists a strong nostalgia for the political greatness of the Roman Republic and Empire, and the hope to restore this greatness was the central political idea that guided him in his dealings with Pope and Emperor, with Cola di Rienzo, and with the various Italian governments. When he was crowned as a poet on the Capitol in 1341, he thought that an ancient Roman honor had been renewed in his own person. Thus he dedicated his historical works and some of his poems to ancient Roman subjects, adopted ancient literary genres for his poems and prose writings, and tried to imitate the language and style of the classical Latin writers.

Among the poets, his greatest admiration was for Vergil, whom he imitated in his poem *Africa,* and of whose *Aeneid* he gave an allegorical interpretation in Book II of his *Secretum,* a practice that followed medieval precedents and was to be continued by later humanists such as Cristoforo Landino. Among the ancient Latin prose writers, Cicero and Seneca were his favorite authors. His letters and his treatise "On the Remedies of Fortune" depend in their style and content on writings composed by Seneca or attributed to him. Even his polemic against dialectic and other branches of scholastic learning, and his emphasis on moral problems, seem to be modeled after the more moderate scepticism that Seneca expresses in his *Moral Epistles* with reference to the subtle dialectic of the older Stoics. Petrarch's taste for moral declamation and for a tearful meditation on death is closer to Seneca than to any other classical writer, and to Seneca he evidently owes those Stoic notions that appear in his writings: the conflict between Virtue and Fortune, the contrast between reason and the four basic passions in the treatise "On the Remedies of Fortune," and the link between virtue and happiness in the *Secretum.*

Even greater is Petrarch's enthusiasm for Cicero. In the treatise "On His Ignorance," Petrarch quotes entire passages from Cicero, and echoing a famous passage from St. Jerome, he calls himself a Ciceronian.[1] To Cicero he owes the form of the dialogue, and much of his information on Greek philosophy. We might even say that Petrarch and other humanists owe to their imitation of Cicero and Seneca, not only the elegance of their style, but also the elusive and at times superficial manner of their reasoning.

Since the main sources of ancient philosophy are Greek rather than Latin, it is important to know what Petrarch's attitude was toward ancient Greek civilization, and how much he knew about it. Like many later humanists, Petrarch was unaware of the extent to which

8

Roman civilization depended upon the Greeks, but he could not fail to notice the numerous references to Greek sources that occurred in the writings of his favorite Roman authors. Hence he made an attempt to learn the Greek language, but apparently he did not progress far enough to read the ancient Greek writers in the original. Yet he acquired a Greek manuscript of Homer, and this manuscript served as a basis of the earliest Latin translation of this poet. The medieval Latin translators from the Greek had concentrated on theology, and on the sciences and Aristotelian philosophy. By suggesting a translation of Homer, Petrarch opened the way for the new humanist interest in classical Greek poetry and literature.

To a certain extent, Petrarch's modest knowledge of Greek and his greater curiosity about Greek literature tended to affect also his philosophical outlook and orientation. Not only did he possess a Greek manuscript of Plato, but he seems to have read some of the dialogues when he took his lessons in that language, and he claims to have read the available Latin translations of Plato, that is, the *Timaeus* and the *Phaedo*. His limited acquaintance with the Platonic dialogues was supplemented by the information on certain Platonic theories that he could find in Cicero and other Latin writers. Thus he knows Plato's theory of the three parts of the soul (reason, courage, and desire),[2] and echoes Plato's notion that man's moral aim should be to purify his soul from the passions.[3]

Yet more important than any acceptance of specific Platonic theories is Petrarch's general conviction that Plato was the greatest of all philosophers, greater than Aristotle, who had been the chief authority of the medieval thinkers. Plato is the prince of philosophy, Petrarch says in his treatise on ignorance;[4] and Plato is praised by the greater men, whereas Aristotle is praised only by the greater number.[5] In the *Triumph of Fame*, where Petrarch mentions the most distinguished philosophers, his words are these: "I turned to the left and saw Plato, who in that group came closest to the goal attained by those to whom this is granted by heaven; then came Aristotle full of a high mind."[6] These words of Petrarch are as expressive of the Renaissance attitude toward Plato as Dante's often-quoted line on "the master of those who know" is of medieval Aristotelianism.[7] Petrarch's "Platonism" was a program and an aspiration rather than a doctrine or a fulfillment, yet it was a beginning and a promise that pointed the way to later developments: to the humanist translations of Plato, and to the Platonist thought of the Florentine Academy. When Raphael painted his School of Athens in the early sixteenth century, Plato had achieved equal stature with Aristotle, and had become as widely known.

As the lines cited from the *Triumph of Fame* have shown, Petrarch gave Aristotle only the second place, but he was far from holding him in contempt. He insists that he knows him, especially his *Ethics*, and he suspects that the original Aristotle may be superior to his medieval translators and commentators. "I confess that I am not much pleased with his style as it appears in Latin, yet I have learned from Greek witnesses and from Cicero that he was quite sweet and elegant and ornate in his own language . . . However, through the inelegance or envy of the translators, he has come down to us in a harsh and rough garb."[8] And in attacking his scholastic opponents, Petrarch charges that "they insist on an Aristotle whom they know only by hearsay . . . and arbitrarily distort even his correct sentences into some awkward meaning."[9] Petrarch did not know that Cicero's praise of Aristotle's style refers to his lost popular writings, and that his extant philosophical works are far from being sweet, elegant, or ornate even in their original Greek text. Yet again Petrarch pointed the way to a new attitude toward Aristotle that was to take shape in the fifteenth and sixteenth centuries, in Ermolao Barbaro, Melanchthon, Jacopo Zabarella, and others. Aristotle was to be studied in the Greek text, and in the company of other Greek philosophers and writers. The medieval translations of Aristotle were to be replaced by new humanist translations (a tremendous undertaking, considering the authority and difficulty of this author, as our English translations of Aristotle may show). And the medieval Arabic and Latin commentators were to give way to the ancient Greek commentators and to those modern Renaissance interpreters who were able to read and understand Aristotle in his original text. Thus Petrarch was the prophet of Renaissance Aristotelianism, as he had been that of Renaissance Platonism.

Although Petrarch opposed the classical authors to the medieval tradition, he was by no means completely detached from his immediate past. The transitional nature of his thought has often been stressed, and there are even a few traces of scholastic philosophy in his writings. Much more important, however, is his attitude toward Christianity. Religious faith and piety occupy a central position in his thought and writings, and there is not the slightest reason to doubt the sincerity of his statements. If there should ever be a conflict between religion and ancient philosophy, he is ready to stand by the teachings of the former. "The highest part of my heart is with Christ," he says.[10] "When it comes to thinking or speaking of religion, that is, of the highest truth, of true happiness and eternal salvation, I certainly am not a Ciceronian or a Platonist, but a Christian."[11] The opinions of all philosophers have but a relative value. "In order to philosophize truly, we must above all love and worship Christ."[12] "To be a true philosopher is nothing but to be a true Christian."[13] The *Secret,* in which Petrarch subjects his most intimate feelings and actions to religious scrutiny, is a thoroughly Christian work. His treatise "On the Remedies of Fortune," with its meditation on death, its humbleness before the future life, and its insistence on the vanity of all earthly goods and evils is equally Christian, and even specifically medieval. His treatise "On the Leisure of the Monks" (*De otio religioso*) belongs to the ascetic tradition, and even his polemic against scholasticism in the name of a genuine and simple religion continues or resumes that strand of medieval religious thought which found expression in Peter Damiani and St. Bernard. In his treatise on his ignorance, Petrarch goes so far as to oppose his own piety to the supposedly irreligious views of his scholastic opponents.

Statements like these have been accepted at their face value by some historians, and have led them to the exaggerated and paradoxical view that Renaissance humanism was in fact a Christian and Catholic reaction against the heretical tendencies inherent in medieval Aristotelianism. Without endorsing this interpretation, we may say that Petrarch gives us a clear example that it was possible for the humanists to reject scholasticism while remaining convinced Christians, and to reconcile their classical learning with their religious faith. He is thus an early, Italian forerunner of that "Christian humanism" which recent historians have emphasized in the work of Colet, Erasmus, More, and other Northern scholars. And curiously enough, whereas a distinguished medievalist has tried to insist that scholastic philosophy is fundamentally Christian, and that the Renaissance is the Middle Ages minus God, one would look in vain for the notion of a Christian philosophy in the writings of the medieval scholastics (for them, including Thomas Aquinas, theology was Christian, and philosophy, Aristotelian, and the problem was how the two could be reconciled); one would find such a notion only in the writings of some early Christian authors, and again in the Christian humanists of the Renaissance, in Petrarch and Erasmus.

In still another way Petrarch's attitude is typical of the manner in which later humanists were to combine their religious faith and their classical learning: for them, the early Christian writers, and especially the Church Fathers, are the Christian classics whom they prefer to read, along with the pagan classics but without the company of the scholastic theologians, and to whom they apply the same scholarly methods of editing, translating, and commenting that they had developed for the study of the ancient authors. In the case of Petrarch, St. Augustine is his favorite Christian writer and occupies a position of unique importance in his thought and work. There are numerous quotations scattered throughout Petrarch's writings, but it is sufficient to mention two notable instances. His *Secret*, in which he scrutinizes his life from the point of view of Christianity, takes the form of a dialogue between the author and St. Augustine, who thus assumes the role of a spiritual guide or of the author's own conscience. And in the famous letter in which Petrarch describes climbing Mont Ventoux, he tells us that when he had arrived at the top of the mountain and wanted to express the feelings the marvelous view had evoked in him, he took St. Augustine's *Confessions* out of his pocket, opened it at random, and hit upon a passage that turned out to be perfectly appropriate for the occasion.[14]

Petrarch was both medieval and modern, and as he once stated himself, he looked backward and forward at the same time, as if placed at the frontier of two countries.[15] Having discussed Petrarch's debt to antiquity and to the Middle Ages, we must now try to describe the modern elements in his thought and attitude. One of them, in my opinion, is the eminently personal, subjective, and, as it were, individualistic character of all his writings. He talks about a variety of things and ideas, but essentially he always talks about himself, about what he has read and felt. This high degree of self-consciousness is especially apparent in his *Secretum* and in his letters, and we might say that Petrarch and most later humanists favored the letter as a literary genre because it enabled them to speak of everything in the first person. The subjective character of Petrarch's writings points to a notable feature of most later humanist thought and literature, a feature that found its culminating expression in one of the last and most philosophical humanists, Michel de Montaigne, who was to state in fact that his own self constituted the chief subject matter of his philosophizing.

Another typical Renaissance attitude was the passion for fame, to which Burckhardt dedicated a few impressive pages of his work. Petrarch condemns this passion both in the *Secret* and in the treatise "On the Remedies of Fortune," but his words in these passages, and the record of his own life, show that he was very much given to it. A further characteristic trait is his curiosity and his love of travel. His experiences and observations during his journeys are recorded in several of his letters, and in the letter about climbing Mont Ventoux, he tells us that he undertook this excursion "only out of the desire to see the unusual altitude of the place."[16] Thus I am unimpressed by the argument of a distinguished historian of science who impugns Petrarch's originality on the grounds that the medieval philosopher Buridan had ascended the very same mountain some years before Petrarch.[17] Originality consists not only in what we do, but also in the manner in which we do it, and in what we think while doing it. Buridan and Petrarch climbed the same mountain, but in a different spirit. Buridan wanted to make meteorological observations, and thus he may have been the forerunner of modern scientific explorers. Petrarch, on the other hand, went only to see and enjoy the wide view, and thus he was the forerunner of modern tourism, a movement to which we must grant at least a considerable economic importance.

There are a few other attitudes that Petrarch bequeathed to modern men of letters, such as his love of solitude and his melancholy. To the praise of solitude he dedicated a whole treatise, "On the Solitary Life" (*De vita solitaria*), and a number of letters, and he never tires of praising the pleasures of the retired life he led in Vaucluse near Avignon, and later in Arquà. Admittedly, the ideal of solitude had been embodied in the tradition of medieval monasticism, and Petrarch does in fact cite the example of monks and hermits. Yet his own ideal is not that of the monk, but that of the scholar and man of letters who withdraws to the countryside, away from the cities, their noise and turbulence, to live undisturbed, at liberty to read and meditate. The most we can say is that Petrarch transformed the monastic ideal of solitude into a secular and literary ideal, and in this form it has been dear to many poets, writers, and scholars to the present day, who still prefer meadows and forests and the shores of lakes and rivers to streets and highways, and even to ivory towers.

Another gift left by Petrarch to modern men of letters was his melancholy. Petrarch was subject to many moods, and he expressed them forcefully in his poems and letters. His special concern with his own melancholy is linked with a famous passage in his *Secretum*. There he speaks of his "acidia" as a mood to which he is frequently subject, and which St. Augustine, his Christian conscience, admonishes him to overcome.[18] Again it has been pointed out that *acidia* appears in the medieval catalogues of vices, and is considered a vice to which monks are especially prone. The medieval term is usually rendered as "sloth." Yet again an aspect that had been characteristic of the monastic life is turned by Petrarch into an experience peculiar to the secular man of letters. At the same time, what had been considered an unmitigated vice, now discloses a positive side, although it is still rejected by Petrarch's religious conscience, as had been his passion for fame. *Acidia* is now defined as suffering mixed with pleasure.[19] This description has led many scholars to think that what Petrarch means by *acidia* is not sloth (how could that be called suffering, let alone suffering mixed with pleasure?), but melancholy.[20] The remark that the suffering is mixed with pleasure contains a precious admission. It tells us that the melancholy scholar and poet suffers, and at the same time enjoys his suffering. Petrarch was to have many followers in this subtle and complex feeling, yet most of them would more readily speak of their suffering than admit it was also enjoyable. Thus Petrarch contributes to secularizing not only the content of learning, but also the personal attitude of the scholar and writer; unlike his successors, however, he hesitates, since he is held back by religious scruples.

Besides these general attitudes, there is at least one more theoretical problem on which Petrarch formulates views akin to those of many later humanists. He keeps asserting that man and his problems should be the main object and concern of thought and philosophy. This is also the justification he gives for his emphasis on moral philosophy, and when he criticizes the scholastic science of his Aristotelian opponents, it is chiefly on the grounds that they raise useless questions, and forget the most important problem, the human soul. When he had reached the top of Mont Ventoux and opened his copy of St. Augustine's *Confessions*, this is the passage he found and quoted: "Men go to admire the heights of mountains, the great floods of the sea, the shores of the ocean, and the orbits of the stars, and neglect themselves."[21] And then he proceeds: "I was angry at myself because I still admired earthly things, I who should have learned long ago from the pagan philosophers [that is, from Seneca] that nothing is admirable but the soul; to it when it is great nothing is great."[22] The words are Petrarch's, and they express his own ideas, but they are characteristically interwoven with quotations from Augustine and Seneca.

Similarly, we read in the treatise on ignorance: "Even if all those things were true, they would have no importance for the happy life. For what would it profit me to know the nature of animals, birds, fish, and snakes, and to ignore or despise the nature of men, the end for which we are born, whence we come and where we go."[23]

Here we find for the first time that emphasis on man which was to receive eloquent expression in the treatises of Facio and Manetti, and to be given a metaphysical and cosmological foundation in the works of Ficino and of Pico. This is why the humanists, beginning with Salutati, adopted the name "humanities" for their studies: to indicate their significance for man and his problems.[24] Yet behind Petrarch's tendency to set moral doctrine against natural science, there are again echoes of Seneca and St. Augustine, and of Cicero's statement that Socrates had brought philosophy down from heaven to earth. When Petrarch speaks of man and his soul, he refers at the same time to the blessed life and eternal salvation, adding a distinctly Christian overtone to his moral and human preoccupation. "It is enough to know as much as suffices for salvation," he says in the treatise "On His Ignorance,"[25] and elsewhere in the same work he insists that the

16

knowledge of God is the main goal of philosophy: "To know God, not the gods, this is the true and highest philosophy."[26] Thus he comes to link the knowledge of man and the knowledge of God in a distinctly Augustinian fashion, and also to discuss an important problem of scholastic philosophy that had its root in Augustine: the question whether the will or the intellect is superior. "It is safer to cultivate a good and pious will than a capable and clear intellect. The object of the will is goodness, the object of the intellect, truth. It is better to will the good than to know the true. . . . Hence those are in error who spend their time in knowing rather than in loving God. For God can in no way be fully known in this life, but He can be loved piously and ardently. . . . It is true that nothing can be loved that is completely unknown. Yet it is enough to know God and virtue up to a certain point (since we cannot know them beyond that point), so long as we know that He is the source of all goodness by Whom and through Whom and in Whom we are good (insofar as we are good), and that virtue is the best thing after God."[27] Thus Petrarch discusses explicitly the scholastic problem of will and intellect, and even follows the Augustinian tradition, as other humanists and Platonists were to do after him, in deciding the question in favor of the superiority of the will over the intellect.

Petrarch, the great poet, writer, and scholar, is clearly an ambiguous and transitional figure when judged by his role in the history of philosophical thought. His thought consists in aspirations rather than developed ideas, but these aspirations were developed by later thinkers, and eventually transformed into more elaborate ideas. His intellectual program may be summed up in the formula which he uses once in the treatise "On His Ignorance": Platonic wisdom, Christian dogma, Ciceronian eloquence.[28] His classical culture, his Christian faith, and his attack against scholasticism are all of a personal, and in a way modern, quality. At the same time, everything he says is pervaded by his classical sources, and often by residual traces of medieval thought.

The old and the new are inextricably intertwined, and we should avoid stressing only the one or the other side, as has often been done. We cannot even say that in terms of his own thought the old is unessential and only the new essential. If we want to do him justice, and to understand his peculiar frame of mind, we must accept the old and the new as equally essential components of his thought and outlook. In this respect, as in so many others, Petrarch is a typical representative of his age, and of the humanist movement. We might even go one step further: Petrarch did not merely anticipate later Renaissance developments because he was unusually talented or perceptive. He also had an active share in bringing them about, because of the enormous prestige he enjoyed among his contemporaries and immediate successors. Like most philosophical (and political) prophets, he was one of those who foresaw the future because they helped to make it.

Valla

The hundred, or hundred and fifty, years after the death of Petrarch constituted a very important period in the history of Italian and European civilization. It was during this period that Renaissance humanism, which had in Petrarch, if not its founder, at least its first great representative, attained its greatest development and influence. The cultural ideals of humanism, as expressed in numerous treatises on education, were put into practice in the schools founded by Guarino, Vittorino, and many others. At the universities, and in many cities that had no university, advanced instruction in the humanistic disciplines, including Greek, was offered more or less regularly, and acquired popularity and prestige. Humanist scholars, or laymen with a humanist training, occupied the leading positions in the chanceries of the papal Curia, of the Florentine Republic, and of many other states and cities, as well as in the councils of princes and republics. Humanists thus came to influence the political thought and life of the period, and the way in which Leonardo Bruni, for many years Florentine chancellor and a leading humanist of his generation, gave literary expression to the republican ideals of his city has deservedly received much attention. In addition to the professional humanists, humanist education produced a large group of cultured statesmen and businessmen who either took an active part in the scholarly and literary work of their fellow humanists, or, by their competent patronage, encouraged them and constituted a sympathetic audience.

The importance of the scholarly and literary activities of the fifteenth-century humanists, at least for their own period, has been generally recognized, but the enormous volume of these activities has hardly been realized, since so much humanist writing remains buried in the unexplored manuscript collections of the Western world. In the field of Latin studies, the humanists rediscovered a number of classical writings and made others better known; preserved and diffused the texts by copying and editing them (the invention of printing occurred during this period); and explained their meaning through learned commentaries. In studying the ancient sources they developed the techniques of textual and historical criticism; studied and restored the orthography, grammar, style, and prosody of classical Latin; expanded the knowledge of ancient history and mythology; and developed such auxiliary disciplines as archaeology and epigraphy. They also introduced the humanist script, which is the basis of our present handwriting and printing, by imitating the Carolingian minuscule, which they mistakenly held to be that of the ancient Romans; and they created the humanist cursive, which is the basis of our italic script.[1]

In the field of Greek studies, the humanists became the heirs of the Byzantine scholars, and were responsible for introducing Greek scholarship into Western Europe. Greek manuscripts were brought from the East to Western libraries; Greek classical texts were copied, printed, and interpreted; and the methods of grammatical and historical scholarship were extended and applied to the classical Greek authors. The bulk of Greek classical literature, largely unknown to the West during the Middle Ages, became well known to Western scholars, partly through the study of the originals in schools and universities, partly through a vast flood of new Latin and vernacular translations. It is no exaggeration to say that the humanists of the fifteenth century laid the ground for the classical, philological, and historical studies of the modern world, and began to develop the sense and method of critical scholarship that have characterized these studies ever since.

Yet the humanists were writers as well as scholars, and in a sense their classical erudition was a handmaid to their literary ambitions. In their work as historiographers, we might say that the two tendencies were of equal weight. But in their voluminous Latin poetry, which comprises all genres from the lyrical and pastoral poem through the historical, mythological, and didactic epic to comedy and tragedy, and which attained special excellence in the composition of elegies and epigrams, classical scholarship figures merely as a necessary tool for the imitation of ancient literary models.

The same is true of the vast prose literature produced by the humanists. It consists of speeches, a genre for which the social and institutional life of the period provided many opportunities; of letters, which were written with literary intentions and constituted a favorite genre because they permitted the writer to talk about anything he pleased, and in a quite personal fashion; and, finally, of dialogues and treatises, which dealt most frequently with questions of moral philosophy, but gradually came to be used for discussing problems of all kinds.

By the middle of the fifteenth century, humanist learning and literature, as it had developed in Italy, began to be a continuous and pervasive influence in other European countries, although, of course, signs of this influence had been evident long before then. The diffusion of Italian humanism was due partly to Italian scholars who had occasion to travel or reside abroad, and partly to foreign students who received their training in Italian schools and universities. This influence is too complex a phenomenon to discuss in detail here; suffice it to say that Renaissance humanism, though originating in Italy, had a strong impact upon the whole of Europe.[2]

Equally important, and perhaps less well understood, is another development of the mid-fifteenth century. At about this time, the impact of humanist learning began to be felt outside the circle of the *studia humanitatis* that constituted its original domain, and to penetrate all other areas of contemporary civilization. It especially affected the other learned disciplines that were taught at the universities, and that had originated in, and derived their traditions from, the high Middle Ages.

As we have seen in the case of Petrarch, humanism from its very beginning was concerned with moral questions. On the other hand, its attitude toward such disciplines as theology, jurisprudence, medicine, logic, natural philosophy, and metaphysics was one of distrust and polemic, and also of ignorance, and largely reflected the rivalry between different disciplines and interests. This situation began to change when practically every educated person had been exposed to humanist training before studying any other discipline. As a result, all kinds of combinations and compromises between humanist and "medieval" professional interests became possible. Apart from the impact of new ideas and new problems, humanist learning had a fermenting effect upon the other disciplines: it introduced new and previously unknown classical sources, treated the old and previously known sources with a new philological and historical method, and introduced new modes of argument, terminology, and literary presentation. It is in this sense that we must understand the humanist element in the theology of Colet and Erasmus and of the Protestant and Catholic reformers, in the jurisprudence of Alciati and of the French school, and in the mathematics and medicine of the sixteenth century.

The impact of humanism on the philosophical thought and literature of the period must be understood along similar lines. One of the important factors is the introduction of new classical sources, and the reinterpretation and re-evaluation of those already known. Among the Latin sources of philosophy, Seneca, Boethius, and most of Cicero had been well known, but were now read and used in a different way; Cicero's *Academica* and the work of Lucretius, not previously known, were introduced, and made a significant addition.

Even more important was the change as it affected the knowledge of the Greek sources of philosophy. Those that had been known before, primarily Aristotle, were retranslated in a different style and terminology, and access was gained to the original Greek texts. Moreover, a vast body of other authors and writings were translated into Latin for the first time: most of the works of Plato and the Neoplatonists, only a few of which had been accessible to the West in the Middle Ages; the Greek commentators of Aristotle, formerly available only in a small selection; Epictetus and Marcus Aurelius, the representatives of late Stoicism; Diogenes Laertius, who offered information on all schools of antiquity, and especially on Epicurus; Sextus Empiricus, the chief source of scepticism, whose shorter treatise only had been translated in the thirteenth century, without attracting much attention; less systematic writers such as Plutarch and Lucian, who were to become great favorites during the Renaissance and afterwards; and, finally, the apocryphal works attributed to Orpheus and Pythagoras, Hermes Trismegistus and Zoroaster, which attained a wide diffusion and served as important channels of transmission for many philosophical and theological ideas of late antiquity. To this we may add the bulk of Greek poetry, oratory, and historiography, of Greek science and pseudo-science, and of early Christian theology, all of which included philosophical ideas, and which was now made completely available and assimilated for the first time.

The way in which this vast new material was used by the humanists and other Renaissance thinkers varied from case to case. Many humanists were eclectics after the manner of Cicero, citing and borrowing ideas and opinions from a variety of authors and schools, guided primarily by their tastes and reading. Others professed allegiance to specific ancient thinkers or traditions, proclaiming themselves new Platonists or Aristotelians, Stoics, Epicureans, or Sceptics, without necessarily following their ancient models as faithfully as they thought they did.

Aside from its classicism, humanism influenced Renaissance thought by its stylistic and literary ideals. The treatise, the dialogue, and later the essay, even the letter and the speech, took the place of the question and the commentary on Aristotle; and the distaste for scholastic arguments and terms led to a freer, if sometimes less precise, expression of ideas and opinions.

Finally, the humanists carried into philosophy their preference for certain problems and topics. If it is hard to see them agree on any specific philosophical opinions, it is easy to note their common orientation in some of their favorite themes, as well as in their classicism and in their style of presentation. The emphasis on moral and human problems, notably on the dignity of man and his place in the universe, seems closely related to the central credo of the humanists. They were also invariably concerned with the problems of free will, fortune, and fate, with the claims of merit and birth in judging a man's nobility, and with the standard topics of ancient ethics. When they ventured outside ethics into the other traditional branches of philosophy, it was their concern to treat the subject with greater clarity and simplicity, and in accordance with their favorite ancient authorities. At the same time, they managed to make some novel contributions of their own, especially in the field of logic.

Valla, whose work we shall now briefly consider, must be viewed within this framework. He is in many ways a typical representative of Italian humanism, but enjoys special fame and distinction, both for his critical spirit and for his contribution to philosophical thought.

Lorenzo Valla was born in Rome in 1407 into a family that originated in Piacenza. After studying in Rome, he taught eloquence at the University of Pavia from 1429 to 1433. After a few years of wandering, he became in 1437 secretary to King Alfonso of Aragon, who was then engaged in the conquest of the Kingdom of Naples. In 1448 he returned to Rome, and became papal secretary and professor at the university. He died in 1457.

Valla's writings reflect a variety of interests. They include letters, a history of King Ferdinand I of Aragon (1445), and translations of the Greek historians Herodotus and Thucydides.³ His invectives reflect the lively controversies in which he was involved with several of his fellow humanists such as Poggio. The famous treatise in which he exposed the apocryphal character of the Donation of Constantine on historical and linguistic grounds (1440) constitutes a notable example of philological criticism, and it was still used in the sixteenth century in the Protestant polemic against the secular power of the papacy. The work was written while Valla was in the service of King Alfonso. He followed it up with an apology, and although he was not forgiven by the reigning pope, he regained the favor of the succeeding popes. Valla's notes on the New Testament represent an early attempt to apply the philological methods of the humanists to the study of Scripture, and they certainly had an influence upon the work of Erasmus, to whom they were known. Valla's letter against the jurist Bartolus (1433) created a scandal that forced him to leave Pavia. It is a document in the history of the battle of the arts, but also an early episode in the development that led to the application of humanist philology to the study of Roman law. Valla's most influential and popular work was the *Elegantiae linguae latinae* (1444), designed to establish the correct usage of the ancient Romans on many points of grammar, phraseology, and style. His aim, as he proudly announces in the Preface, was to restore the Latin language to the glory and purity that marked it before its corruption by the barbarians.⁴ The work was a major effort in the history of humanist philology, and it served as a textbook of Latin stylistics for many centuries down to about 1800.

Valla's contribution to philosophy is largely contained in three works: a fairly short dialogue, "On Free Will" (*De libero arbitrio,* written between 1435 and 1443); a much longer dialogue, "On Pleasure" (*De voluptate,* or *De vero bono,* 1431–32); and a work entitled "Dialectical Disputations" (*Dialecticae disputationes,* 1439). Let us consider each of them in turn.

In the first, starting from a statement of Boethius,[5] Valla sets out to answer the question whether God's foreknowledge and the freedom of the human will are compatible. Aiming at an affirmative answer, he argues that the possibility of an event does not necessarily involve its actual occurrence, and that previous knowledge of a future event, even on the part of God, must not be considered a cause of that event. It is true that in God there is no separation of His wisdom from His will and power, yet there certainly is a distinction between them. To illustrate this distinction, Valla uses the pagan gods as allegories for the different powers or attributes of the Christian God. Apollo, representing God's foreknowledge and power of prediction, is distinct from Jupiter, who represents His will and His power over fate. Apollo can foresee and predict all future events without error, but he does not cause them, and therefore his prediction is compatible with the free will of the human agents who will produce the events.

In this way the initial question seems to have been resolved in a satisfactory fashion, but it immediately re-emerges on a different level. For there is no doubt that God's will and power cause all things and events, including human beings and their inclinations. Thus we are driven to ask how God's will can be reconciled with the free will of human beings, since it is God Who hardens man's will or shows him mercy. In other words, Valla has shown that divine providence and human free will are compatible, but he has not answered the question whether divine predestination leaves any room for human free will. In fact, he refuses to answer this second question, alleging that he had promised to answer only the first. When he is pressed, he replies that God's will is a mystery hidden from men and angels alike, and that we should accept it on the basis of faith. We should strive for Christian humbleness rather than for the pride of philosophy, and abandon our curiosity about a question we cannot answer.[6]

Valla shows considerable acumen in the first part of the dialogue, and it is significant that it was to this work Leibniz referred when he termed Valla not merely a humanist, but a philosopher.[7] Yet I cannot agree with those historians who interpret the work as a monument of secular and rational thought. Valla clearly subordinates philosophy to faith: in the Preface he even goes so far as to say that religion and theology should not rely on the support of philosophy; that theologians should cease to treat philosophy as the sister, or even the patron, of theology; that philosophy is not useful, but harmful, to religion, and has been the cause of many heresies.[8] To be sure, Valla means by philosophy the scholastic philosophy of the medieval tradition; it remains a fact, however, that he does not reject it in the name of a new and better philosophy, but in the name of religion and faith.

More interesting, and in a way more important, is the longer dialogue, in three books, which Valla entitled at first "On Pleasure" (*De voluptate,* 1431), and which he later preferred to call "On the True Good" (*De vero bono,* 1432). This work underwent more than one revision at the hands of its author, but these changes do not seem to have affected its substance. A critical edition of the text has been promised for some time, but at the moment we still depend on the vulgate text of the sixteenth-century editions, which seems to be rather unreliable in its wording.[9]

In this version, the best known and most accessible, Valla discusses the question of what constitutes the true good for human beings, a problem that had been central to most ancient treatises on ethics, and that was familiar to Valla especially from Cicero's *De finibus.* Valla's work takes the form of a dialogue between spokesmen for three different views on the matter. The first character, Leonardus, defends a position that Valla identifies as Stoic. His speech, which occupies the first eight chapters of the first book, identifies the highest good with moral virtue, a view which does indeed correspond to that of the ancient Stoics. Yet whereas the Stoics considered nature and providence perfect, Leonardus complains about the wrath and injustice of nature, which has made virtue so rare and difficult to attain that man,

27

on account of his higher goal, is left in an unhappier state than the animals (chs. 2–8).

The second and longest speech, which occupies the remainder of the first book and the whole of the second, is made by Antonius, who refutes the Stoics and defends the Epicureans. According to his view, which differs in many ways from the authentic position of Epicurus, the true good of man does not consist in moral virtue, but in pleasure, which is identified throughout with usefulness (ch. 16). In defending this position, Antonius passes in review the goods of fortune, of the body and of the soul, and shows that they are all related to the pleasures of either the body or the soul (chs. 19–33). Pleasure alone is in accordance with nature, and, far from being considered inferior to the virtues, should be regarded as their ruler (ch. 34). Every pleasure is good, Antonius declares; in a bold defense of erotic pleasures, he even advocates adultery and the common ownership of women after the manner of Plato's *Republic,* and entirely rejects the monastic ideal of virginity (chs. 38–46).

Stoic virtue has no meaning; it is an imaginary thing. Fame is a useless ideal, and if it is given any positive value, it must be considered a kind of pleasure (Bk. II, chs. 12–21). What good men pursue is usefulness rather than virtue (ch. 28). Usefulness, not virtue, is the aim of all laws, for he who obeys the laws out of fear cannot be considered virtuous in his soul (ch. 30). Even the contemplative life and the tranquillity of the mind, which have been set up as ideals by many philosophers, are desired only for the sake of the pleasures that go with them (chs. 36–37).

In concluding his speech, Antonius insists that man is nothing but an animal, and has no existence after death. Hence the belief in future rewards and punishments must be rejected. Human good consists in the pleasures that may be attained during the present life. If we distinguish between virtues and vices, tending to pursue the former and avoid the latter, we do so because the virtues provide us with higher and more lasting pleasures (chs. 38–39).

Valla

The last book of the dialogue is occupied largely by the speech of Nicolaus, who criticizes both preceding speakers and expresses a third view, which is presented as the Christian doctrine. It is not true, he argues, that evil pleases us more than good, for man always desires the good and avoids evil, and his will is spontaneously directed toward the good as our eyes are turned toward the light (Bk. III, chs. 2–3). Yet pleasure itself is a good, and hence a legitimate goal for us. When Antonius defended the Epicurean position, Nicolaus argues, he did not express his real opinion, but spoke jokingly; for it is contrary to the Christian faith to deny the afterlife, or to put man on a level with the animals, and Antonius in real life is a good Christian. Leonardus, by contrast, spoke in earnest when defending the Stoic position, but was prompted to do so by an excessive admiration for the ancients. We should praise the ancients for their knowledge, but not for their morals. The Stoic doctrine is not compatible with Christianity, for it puts nature in the place of Christ (ch. 6).

Thus the virtues of the Stoics are really vices, and Antonius was right to criticize Stoic virtue. According to St. Paul, we cannot serve God or renounce the goods of the present life without the hope of a future reward, and all human virtues are useless without the theological virtues of faith, hope, and Christian love. The Stoic sage possesses no peace of mind, and his virtue is actually full of trouble. If we were to deny the possibility of rewards after death, as the ancient philosophers did, the doctrine of Epicurus should be preferred to that of the Stoics. For Stoic virtue is desired for its own sake; its connection with God has been forgotten, and it is therefore a false virtue. The Epicureans, on the other hand, pursue virtue for the sake of usefulness, and are thus superior. The Christians, finally, desire virtue for the sake of future happiness, and for this reason they are superior to both the Stoics and the Epicureans (chs. 7–8).

This future happiness at which the Christians aim is also a kind of pleasure, and for this reason the Epicureans come closer to the target

29

than the Stoics. Not virtue, but pleasure, must be desired—both by those who wish to enjoy it in this life and by those who expect to enjoy it in the next. For pleasure is of two kinds, the one now on earth, the other later in heaven. The one is the mother of vice, the other of virtue. Hence we must abstain from the one if we want to enjoy the other. We can attain either one, but we cannot attain both together, for they are contrary to each other.[10] The pleasure here on earth is uncertain and passing; the other pleasure is assured and lasting. When our mind is set on its right course toward this future happiness, it experiences already in this present life a pleasure that comes from the hope and expectation of future felicity. Nothing is done well without pleasure, and there is no merit in him who serves God obediently but not gladly, for God likes a glad servant (ch. 9).

Now, the chief means for attaining future beatitude is virtue, but it is the virtue of the Christians, not of the philosophers, that is, of the Stoics. Virtue and happiness, however, must be distinguished. The highest good is identical with pleasure, and virtue as well as many other things is called good only insofar as it produces the good, that is, pleasure. Apart from this connection with pleasure and usefulness, the virtue of the philosophers must be considered an evil (ch. 11).

In this way the Stoics and Epicureans are both refuted, and the highest good is found, not in any of the philosophical doctrines, but in the Christian religion. For when we succeed in overcoming our earthly passions, our soul will ascend to heaven, whereas the souls of the wicked will descend to hell. We shall thus enjoy an eternal pleasure far more excellent than any of the earthly pleasures praised by Antonius. For our life on earth is necessarily beset with trouble and misery (chs. 14–15).

Nicolaus then praises the beauty of the visible world, and states that it was created for the sake of man so that through the contemplation of the universe he may lift himself toward the expectation of a higher life (ch. 16). At the end of his speech, Nicolaus gives a description of the future life, basing himself, he says, not on any knowledge, but on faith and imagination.[11] When the soul has risen to heaven, it will enjoy a variety of pleasures. He insists that the heavenly life includes corporeal pleasures more intense than any we may experience on earth, but adds that heaven's intellectual pleasures are still more intense, and that the enjoyment attained by the soul in heaven is thus complete and perfect in every way (chs. 25–28). The speech, and with it the dialogue, ends with a hymn-like description of the triumphal entry of the soul into heaven, where it is received by Christ and the Virgin, by the choirs of the angels, and by its own friends and relatives (ch. 29).

The meaning of the dialogue, and the ethical and philosophical position that Valla intended to express in this work, has been interpreted in two entirely different ways. Some historians are inclined to dismiss the third book as a transparent attempt on Valla's part to escape censure and to disguise his true opinion. They take the long speech of Antonius as the statement of Valla's real views, and tend to regard the bold defense of erotic pleasure, and the denial of a future life, as a characteristic expression of Renaissance thought. Other interpreters, and I am inclined to side with them, have taken a very different stand on the matter.

There is no doubt that Valla is trying to build up the Epicurean position at the expense of the Stoic, and that he is presenting Antonius's bold and shocking remarks with gusto. Yet there is no evidence that he adopted in real life, or in his other writings, a view similar to that of Antonius, or that he was devoid of religious faith. I rather think that Nicolaus's speech in the third book comes close to representing Valla's real views, and am inclined to take him at his word when he says through Nicolaus that he prefers the Epicurean to the Stoic position (as he understands them) because the former comes nearer to the Christian doctrine (as he chooses to present it).

This view is supported by the organization of the dialogue, in which the third book constitutes a kind of climax, and presents a solution of the problem through which the positions of the first two speakers are both refuted and overcome. Moreover, the tone of the third speech is far too eloquent and emphatic to be dismissed as a mere attempt at avoiding offense, and the manner in which the Christian position is presented is so personal and unconventional that it may very well be considered sincere for that very reason. Furthermore, it is in the third book that we find a theory peculiar to Valla, a theory he advances also in another work, the *Dialectic,* and in an entirely different context. In both passages Valla criticizes the well-known doctrine of Aristotle that each moral virtue is a mean between two opposite vices, and asserts instead that each virtue has but one opposite vice. For example, for Valla courage is not a mean between boldness and cowardice, as Aristotle claims, but courage is opposed to cowardice, and prudence to boldness.[12] Finally, in the Preface to the dialogue "On the True Good," where Valla evidently speaks in his own name, and tries to explain to the reader the intent of his work, he clearly identifies the position of the third book as his own. Do you really say that pleasure is the true good? Yes, I do; and I shall assert that nothing but pleasure is good, and I have decided to assume and to prove its cause. Yet this true good is of two kinds, one in this life, the other in the future life. We prefer the latter to the former, but the former to the virtue of the philosophers. We shall set out to refute the Stoics, the defenders of virtue, and assume the defense of the Epicureans, and in this way we shall also defend the Christian religion.[13]

For these reasons I think we may regard Nicolaus as the spokesman for Valla's own opinion. Valla expresses his preference for the Epicureans over the Stoics, but considers the Christians superior to both of them. Yet it is a peculiar conception of Christianity that Valla defends. In many ways it is colored by Epicureanism, almost a vulgarized Epicureanism. The emphasis given to pleasure, and even to corporeal pleasure, in the future life of the Christian is characteristic of a view we may call Christian Epicureanism. Valla was not the first, or the only, Renaissance thinker who attempted to restate Epicurean-ism, and to reconcile it with Christianity.[14] This tendency to Chris-tianize Epicureanism, as it were, to emphasize its affinity with Chris-tianity, forms an interesting contrast with the attitude of the early Christian writers, who were almost unanimous in condemning Epi-cureanism, while showing much more tolerance for Stoicism and some other schools of ancient philosophy. Yet for the very reason that Valla's conception of Christianity is strange and unconventional, I am inclined to consider it sincere.

On the relation between philosophy and religion, Valla does not express himself any more positively in this work than he had done in the dialogue "On Free Will." He makes no effort to confirm religion through philosophy. When he describes the afterlife, he relies on faith and imagination, not on knowledge. In the Preface to the dialogue "On the True Good," he states that it is his purpose to defend religion against the doubts of some modern philosophers,[15] and at one point in the third book he rejects all philosophers without exception.[16] Whenever he recognizes something besides religion, it is not philos-ophy but eloquence. He compares philosophy to a private or sergeant serving under oratory as a general,[17] and the orators, we are told, know much better than the dialecticians how to discuss a problem.[18] Oratory is called the queen of things,[19] and in the last chapter of the third book Antonius and Nicolaus are praised as good orators.[20] With this remark, the entire work seems to assume the appearance of a rhetorical exer-cise, but with all the dignity and value that rhetoric and oratory possess for a convinced humanist.

The last of Valla's three main philosophical works constitutes per-haps his most significant contribution to philosophical thought. Since it is too intricate and technical to describe in detail here, we must be content with a brief indication of its place in the general history of Renaissance thought. "Dialectical Disputations" (*Dialecticae dispu-tationes,* 1439) is divided into three books. In the Preface, Valla announces as his task the reconstruction (*reconcinnatio*) of dialectic and of the foundations of all philosophy, and criticizes in particular the modern Aristotelians, claiming for himself the freedom to dissent from Aristotle.

Broadly speaking, the three books deal respectively with concepts, propositions, and forms of conclusion. Within this framework, however, Valla discusses a great number of specific doctrines, beginning with the categories and the transcendentals, and proposes everywhere interesting new terms and distinctions in the place of the traditional ones, digressing quite often into philosophical disciplines other than logic. There is an obvious tendency to simplify doctrines that he considers unnecessarily complicated. Against the "barbaric" terminology of the scholastic philosophers, he appeals to the grammar and usage of classical Latin, which he prefers even to that of ancient Greek.[21] One is reminded of present-day attempts to base philosophy and especially logic on ordinary language, with the only difference that this ordinary language for Valla is not contemporary English but classical Latin, which is at least several steps closer to ancient Greek, the true fountainhead of all philosophical discourse in the Western world.

In his theory of arguments and of the forms of conclusion, Valla repeatedly borrows from Quintilian, an author whom he praises very highly. This attempt to introduce the rhetorician Quintilian as a new authority into dialectic illustrates a typical humanist tendency to subordinate logic to rhetoric. Valla also remarks at the beginning of the second book that dialectic, in comparison with rhetoric, is a rather short and easy topic that has been made artificially complicated by modern writers on the subject.[22] In other words, Valla's dialectic is an attempt to reform the logic of Aristotle and of the late scholastics, and the purpose of this reform is to simplify logic as a whole, to reduce it to classical Latin usage, and to link it with, if not reduce it to, the discipline of rhetoric, which constituted the professional core and favorite subject of humanist learning.

It would be an exaggeration to claim that Valla's dialectic brought about a lasting reform of that discipline, or that he found many followers for the specific notions and doctrines he proposed. Yet his work is historically important as a first attempt to apply the standards of humanist thought and learning to a philosophical discipline other than ethics. In his general effort to overthrow the logic of late scholasticism and to replace it with a new and simplified logic that was allied with rhetoric and grammar, Valla found a number of important successors during the later Renaissance. It is sufficient to mention Rudolph Agricola, Marius Nizolius, and, above all, Peter Ramus, who attained the success vainly hoped for by his predecessors. For the system formulated by Ramus was adopted by followers in many countries for several centuries, as we have learned from recent studies, and his influence extended not only to Germany and England but to America as well.[23] Keeping these later developments in mind, we might say that among all philosophical disciplines outside of ethics, logic was the most strongly affected by the impact of Renaissance humanism. To be sure, the value of this impact has been questioned by many historians of logic, but its very extent in space and time should give us pause, and point up the need for further study.

Lorenzo Valla, as I hope to have shown, not only was a distinguished humanist, but also made significant contributions to philosophical thought, in spite of his ambiguous attitude toward philosophy. The same may be said of several other, though by no means of all, Renaissance humanists. Valla's work is of special interest because of the authority and influence it had in the rest of Europe, forming a bridge, as it were, between Italian and Northern humanism.

Of the thinkers discussed in these lectures, Valla is the last who may be classified without qualification as a humanist, although most of the others, as we shall see, were more or less affected by humanist learning. In thus taking leave of Renaissance humanism, I should like to state that I do not agree with those historians who claim that humanism vanished from the scene, in Italy and in the North, with the beginning of the sixteenth century, or with the rise of the Reformation. In fact, the sixteenth century witnessed a continuous flowering of humanist learning all over Europe on a very large scale, and the influence of humanism penetrated deeply into all areas of civilization, without regard to the religious and professional divisions prevalent at the time. Some of the greatest humanists belong to the sixteenth century, and several of them left their mark on the history of thought. The names of Erasmus, Vives, Fracastoro, Montaigne, and Lipsius should be sufficient to dispel the notion that during the later Renaissance humanism lost its vitality, or its power to shape and influence the thought of writers and of readers.

3

Ficino

The Platonism of the Florentine Academy, to which this and the next chapter are dedicated, was closely linked in more than one way with the humanist movement. Its leader, Marsilio Ficino, to whom we shall first direct our attention, had enjoyed an excellent training in the classical languages and literatures, and was extremely well-read in the Greek as well as the Latin sources of ancient philosophy. He wrote a fluent, if not an elegant, Latin style, which had a distinctive personal note and satisfied most, if not all, of his fastidious contemporaries. He cultivated such literary genres as the treatise, the dialogue, the oration, and the letter, collected his correspondence, and dealt on equal terms with many leading humanists of his time. His scholarly activity as a translator and commentator of Plato, Plotinus, and other Greek philosophical writers may be regarded as a continuation of the work done by his humanist predecessors. His eclecticism, as well as his effort to revive Platonic philosophy, seems to correspond to the way in which other humanist thinkers used the philosophical heritage of classical antiquity. The edifying tone that characterizes many of his letters reminds one more than once of the letters of Seneca or Petrarch. His preoccupation with the dignity of man and his place in the universe, and with fortune and fate, prompts him to take up several of the favorite themes of early humanist literature.

In spite of all these undeniable facts, I cannot agree with those historians who want to see in Ficino and Renaissance Platonism nothing but a special sector or phase of humanism; I prefer to consider Renaissance Platonism a distinct movement within the broader context of Renaissance philosophy. For it is not enough to say that the Florentine Academy flourished a generation or half a century after the great period of early humanism to which Valla still belonged, or that the second half of the fifteenth century was characterized by religious and metaphysical interests that were alien to the earlier period. Religious and philosophical interests were also alive before the middle of the fifteenth century, although they were not shared by some of the humanists, and, vice versa, there were many humanists during the second half of the fifteenth century who did not share these interests either. The conclusion seems to be unavoidable that the Platonism represented by Ficino and his Academy occupied a different place in the intellectual life of the period.

As a matter of fact, Ficino's Platonism was nourished by many sources and antecedents unrelated to humanism; its connection with earlier humanism represents only one of the many facets that compose its highly diversified thought. First of all, the Florentine Academy constitutes a new phase in the long and complex history of the Platonic tradition, and Ficino was quite conscious of being an heir and standard-bearer of that tradition. His sources include not only the writings of Plato himself and of the ancient Platonists whom we usually call Neoplatonists, but also those attributed to Hermes Trismegistus and Zoroaster, Orpheus and Pythagoras, which modern scholarship has recognized as apocryphal products of late antiquity, but which Ficino, like many of his predecessors and contemporaries, considered venerable witnesses of a very old pagan philosophy and theology that preceded and inspired Plato and his disciples. Ficino was aware, too, that Platonism had its followers among the ancient Latin writers, the early Church authors, and the medieval Arabic and Latin philosophers: for example, Boethius and Calcidius, Dionysius the Areopagite and St. Augustine, Avicenna and Alfarabi, Henry of Ghent and Duns Scotus, and, in his own century, Bessarion and Cusanus. We know from Ficino's writings that many, if not all, of these authors were more or less well known to him. The degree to which he was indebted to any one of them, and the content and importance of these debts in relation to each other and to his own originality, are of course moot questions, which in many instances have not yet been properly examined or answered. Yet it is quite evident that at least Plato and Plotinus, the writings attributed to Zoroaster and Hermes, and the philosophical works of St. Augustine left a deep impression upon his thought. To these names we may add the Byzantine Platonist Gemistos Plethon, who, according to Ficino's own report, gave to Cosimo de' Medici the idea of founding a Platonic Academy in Florence, an idea that was to find its fulfillment many years later through Ficino himself.

Besides early humanism, and ancient and medieval Platonism, Ficino absorbed a good many other influences that are often overlooked because they do not fit the label of Platonism. During an early period of his development, he was impressed by the Epicureanism of Lucretius, and a trace of this influence persisted throughout his life. He attended courses in Aristotelian philosophy at the University of Florence, and his acquaintance with the texts and methods of scholasticism appears not only in some of his early writings, which have been published in recent years, but also in the terminology and method of reasoning of his mature writings, in the use he makes of Aristotle and his Arabic commentators, and even in the structure of his main work, the *Platonic Theology*, which takes the form of a *summa* on the immortality of the soul and offers different series of arguments in support of its main thesis. He had a direct acquaintance with at least some of the writings of Thomas Aquinas, and followed the great scholastic thinker in many statements and arguments; but lest we are tempted to call him a Thomist, we should remember that he came to side with

Ficino

Scotus against Thomas on one of the crucial issues dividing them, the question of whether the will or the intellect was superior. As a good citizen of Florence, Ficino wrote or rewrote several of his works in the Tuscan vernacular; and as a priest, he was imbued not only with the somewhat diluted scholastic theology characteristic of his time and country, but also with the popular religious literature that developed around the lay fraternities which flourished in the Florence of his youth. He was the son of a surgeon, and had himself studied medicine, and he had a more than common knowledge of astrology, as was customary among the physicians of his period. Finally, he had a genuine enthusiasm for cosmological and metaphysical speculation, and managed to formulate ideas and theories that made a deep impact upon the thought of his time and several subsequent centuries.

Marsilio Ficino was born in Figline near Florence in 1433. He received his education in Florence, first in the humanities and then in philosophy and medicine, but he does not seem to have obtained an academic degree. His earliest philosophical work was composed in 1454, and several other writings date from the following years. We know that he began to study Greek around 1456, with the express purpose of examining the original sources of Platonic philosophy, and he soon made his first attempts to translate some philosophical texts into Latin. In 1462, Cosimo de' Medici gave him a house in Careggi near Florence, and placed several Greek manuscripts at his disposal, and this is usually regarded as the date when the Platonic Academy of Florence was founded. Ficino soon completed his translation of the Hermetic writings (1463), which was destined to have a very wide diffusion, and then began to translate Plato's dialogues, and had completed at least ten of them by the time Cosimo died in 1464.

During the following years, Ficino finished his translation of Plato (before 1469), which was the first complete version of this author into any Western language. In 1469, he wrote his famous commentary on Plato's *Symposium*, and between 1469 and 1474, his chief philosophical work, the *Platonic Theology* (*Theologia Platonica*). Toward the end of 1473, he became a priest, probably having taken minor orders at an early date, and we know that he subsequently held several ecclesiastic benefices, and eventually became a canon of Florence Cathedral. Around 1473 he began to collect his letters, and his life and activities are best known to us for the twenty odd years following this date. The collection was carefully edited by the author (1495), and it includes many smaller philosophical treatises composed at different periods of his life. After 1484, Ficino was occupied for many years with his translation and commentary of Plotinus, which was printed in 1492. During his last years, he wrote several more translations, commentaries, and treatises. Having been closely associated with several generations of the Medici family, he seems to have retired to the country after their expulsion from Florence in 1494. He died in 1499, and was honored by a funeral oration delivered by a chancellor of the Republic; later, a monument in his memory was erected in the Cathedral of Florence.

Ficino's writings, sources, and interests having been mentioned, it remains for us to say a few words about the famous Platonic Academy of which he was the head and guiding spirit for many years. The name "Academy" was used by Ficino and his contemporaries, but it is now generally agreed that this was a rather loosely organized circle of friends, rather than a firmly established institution in the manner of the academies of the following centuries. Ficino wanted his Academy to take the form of a spiritual community, and he may have been influenced in this aim by the lay religious associations of his time, as well as by the imagined model of Plato's Academy and other ancient philosophical schools. There were, we know, informal discussions with the older members of the circle, and on at least two occasions, Plato's birthday was celebrated with a banquet at which each participant gave a philosophical speech. There were recitals, before a small circle, of edifying orations that Ficino called declamations, private readings of Plato and other texts with one or a few younger disciples, and public lectures on Plato and Plotinus delivered in a church or an adjacent auditorium. Distinguished visitors from other Italian cities or abroad called upon Ficino or participated in the meetings, and Ficino's correspondence served as a conscious vehicle both for maintaining contact with the members of the Academy and for arousing the interest of strangers in its activities. The catalogue of his pupils, which he gives in one of his letters, and the list of the persons with whom he was in correspondence, whom he mentions, or who owned the manuscripts and printed editions of his writings are ample evidence of the wide influence he exerted during his lifetime, and of the respect in which his writings and other activities were held, not only in Florence, but also in the rest of Italy and in most of Europe.

Marsilio Ficino's writings, especially his *Platonic Theology* and his letters, present a highly complex system of ideas, his philosophical opinions being embroidered, as it were, with similes and allegories, and with lengthy quotations from his favorite authors. The best we can hope to do in a short chapter is to mention a few of his more important or influential doctrines.

Unlike his humanist predecessors, Ficino attempted to give an elaborate description of the universe. He inherited from his Neoplatonic and medieval sources the conception of the universe as a great hierarchy in which each being occupies its place, and has its degree of perfection, beginning with God at the top, and descending through the orders of the angels and souls, the celestial and elementary spheres, the various species of animals, plants and minerals, down to shapeless prime matter. Yet it is not enough to say, as is often done, that Ficino's cosmology consists in a Neoplatonic hierarchy; for on closer examination it appears that his hierarchy differs in several significant details from those of his predecessors. In the first place, it is arranged in a scheme of five basic substances: God, the angelic mind, the rational soul, quality, and body, and this scheme differs in several ways from that of Plotinus, to which it otherwise comes closest. Aside from subtle differences in the meaning of the various terms, quality does not constitute a separate level of being for Plotinus, who assigns instead separate places to the sensitive and vegetative faculties of the soul. It can be shown that Ficino intentionally revised the Plotinian scheme, partly to make it more symmetrical, and partly to assign the privileged place in its center to the human soul, thus giving a kind of metaphysical setting and sanction to the doctrine of the dignity of man, a doctrine he inherited from his humanist predecessors. The soul is truly the mean of all things created by God, he tells us. It is in the middle between higher and lower beings, sharing some of its attributes with the former, and some with the latter.[1]

Yet Ficino is not satisfied with a static hierarchy in which each degree merely stands besides the others, and in which their relation consists only in a continuous gradation of attributes. He is also convinced that the universe must have a dynamic unity, and that its various parts and degrees are held together by active forces and affinities. For this reason, he revived the Neoplatonic doctrine of the world soul, and made astrology a part of a natural system of mutual influences. Now since for Ficino thought has an active influence upon its objects, and since love, according to Plato's *Symposium,* is an active force that binds all things together, and since the human soul extends its thought and love to all things from the highest to the lowest, the soul becomes once more, and in a new sense, the center of the universe. The soul is the greatest of all miracles in nature, for it combines all things, is the center of all things, and possesses the forces of all. Therefore it may be rightly called the center of nature, the middle term of all things, the bond and juncture of the universe.[2]

Ficino's cosmology, which was very influential for some time, is interesting, but it constitutes only one side of his philosophical thought. The other, even more profound, component is his analysis, based on direct inner experience, of the spiritual or contemplative life, an analysis that links him with some of the medieval mystics, and again with Neoplatonism. In the face of our ordinary daily experiences, our mind finds itself in a state of continuous unrest and dissatisfaction. However, it is capable of turning away from the body and the external world, and of concentrating upon its own inner substance. Thus purifying itself from things external, the soul enters the contemplative life and attains a higher knowledge, discovering the incorporeal or intelligible world that is closed to it while engaged in ordinary experience and in the troubles of the external life. Ficino interprets this contemplative life as a gradual ascent of the soul toward always higher degrees of truth and being, an ascent that finally culminates in the immediate knowledge and vision of God. This knowledge of God represents the ultimate goal of human life and existence; in it alone the unrest of our mind is satisfied, and all other modes and degrees of human life and knowledge must be understood as more or less direct or conscious preparations for this ultimate end. In accordance with Plotinus, Ficino is convinced that this highest experience can be attained during the present life, at least by a few privileged persons and for a short while, although he never explicitly claims to have attained this state himself.[3]

In describing the various stages and ultimate goal of inner experience, Ficino uses a twofold terminology, and in this he is influenced by St. Augustine and by the medieval philosophers. The ascent of the soul toward God is accomplished with the help of two wings, the intellect and the will, and thus the knowledge of God is accompanied and paralleled on each level by the love of God, and the ultimate vision by an act of enjoyment. Ficino also considers the question of whether intellect and knowledge or will and love are more important in this process, and although he seems to come to different conclusions in different parts of his writings, he leans on the whole toward the superiority of will and love over intellect and knowledge.[4] Yet the question is not so important for him as might be expected, since he regards the knowledge of God and the love of God as merely two different aspects or interpretations of the same basic experience, namely the contemplative ascent of the soul toward its ultimate goal.

This experience, and the manner in which it is interpreted, holds the key to Ficino's metaphysics and to his ethics alike. It is the inner ascent of contemplation, through which the reality of incorporeal things, of the ideas and of God Himself, is discovered and verified. Moreover, since this inner ascent constitutes the basic task of human existence, Ficino is not interested in specific moral precepts or in casuistry, but only in the general identification of the human good and man's moral excellence with the inner life. His whole moral doctrine, as expressed in his letters, may be said to be a reduction of all specific rules to a praise of the contemplative life. He who has attained this life is exempt from the blows of fortune, and, animated by his inner certainty and insight, he will know and do the right thing under any given circumstances.[5]

Intimately related to the doctrine of the contemplative life are two other theories of Ficino, both of great historical importance, namely his theory of the immortality of the soul and his theory of Platonic love.

The immortality of the soul constitutes the main theme of Ficino's chief philosophical work, the *Platonic Theology*, which carries the subtitle "On the Immortality of the Souls," and which consists for the most part of a series of arguments in support of immortality. It also appears from a famous passage twice repeated in Ficino's writings that he considered this doctrine the central tenet of his Platonism, placing him in direct contrast with the teachings of the Aristotelian philosophers of his time.[6] Now it is true that the immortality of the soul had been defended by Plato and Plotinus, by Augustine and many other Christian writers, and that Ficino borrowed many specific arguments from these predecessors. It may also be granted that Averroes' doctrine of the unity of the intellect in all men, which had been widely accepted or discussed by the Aristotelian philosophers from the thirteenth to the fifteenth century, made a defense of individual immortality imperative. We may add that the humanists had attached great importance to the individual human being, his experiences and his opinions, and that the belief in personal immortality was, as it were, a metaphysical counterpart of this individualism, and an extension of it into another dimension.[7]

Yet in the case of Ficino, it seems evident that the doctrine of immortality was a necessary complement and consequence of his interpretation of human existence and of the goal of human life. If it is our basic task to ascend, through a series of degrees, to the immediate vision and enjoyment of God, we must postulate that this ultimate goal will be attained, not merely by a few persons and for a short while, but by a great number of human beings and for ever. Otherwise man's effort to attain this ultimate end would be in vain, and the very end for which he had been destined would remain without fulfillment. Thus man would be unhappier than the animals, which do attain their natural ends, and this would be inconsistent with the dignity of the place man occupies in the universe. Moreover, a natural end corresponding to a natural desire implanted in all men could not be attained, and this would be in contrast with the perfection of the order of nature, and with the wisdom of God who created this order. In his *Platonic Theology*, and in other parts of his writings, Ficino never tires of repeating these and similar arguments; it seems obvious that they reflect the real intent and motivation of his thought. For his whole interpretation of human life as a contemplative ascent toward God would lose its meaning unless this ascent were to find its permanent fulfillment in the eternal afterlife of the immortal soul. This alone, it seems to me, explains why the doctrine of immortality assumes such a central place for him. All other arguments he uses are merely auxiliary to this central one.[8]

Ficino's doctrine of immortality, and his arguments for it, made a profound impression on many thinkers of the sixteenth century, and it may well be due to his indirect influence that the immortality of the soul was formally pronounced a dogma of the Catholic Church at the Lateran Council of 1512.

Of equal historical importance, although of a different character, is Ficino's doctrine of human love. In this doctrine, as in many others, Ficino combined elements from several different sources and traditions. He took over and reinterpreted Plato's theory of love as expressed in the *Symposium* and *Phaedrus,* and combined it with some other ancient theories of friendship that were known to him primarily from Aristotle and Cicero; he tried to identify it with the Christian love (*charitas*) praised by St. Paul; and he even added some touches from the tradition of medieval courtly love as it was known to him through Guido Cavalcanti, Dante, and other early Tuscan poets. This doctrine, which exercised a tremendous influence during the sixteenth century, and for which Ficino himself coined the terms Platonic and Socratic love, was first expressed by him in his commentary on Plato's *Symposium*, and then further developed in many of his letters and other writings. The name "Platonic love" means love as described by Plato, according to Ficino's interpretation. More frequently, Ficino speaks of it as divine love. The basic point is that he regards love for another human being as merely a preparation, more or less conscious, for the love of God, which constitutes the real goal and true content of human desire, and which is merely turned toward persons and things by the reflected splendor of divine goodness and beauty as it may appear in them. He insists that true love and friendship is always mutual. A genuine relationship between two people is a communion founded on what is essential in man: that is, it is based in each of them on his original love for God. There can never be two friends only; there must always be three, two human beings and one God. God alone is the insoluble bond and perpetual guardian of any true friendship, for a true lover loves the other person solely for the sake of God. In other words, true love and friendship between several persons is derived from the love of the individual for God, and it is thus reduced to the basic phenomenon of the inner ascent, which constitutes the core of Ficino's philosophy.[9]

It appears from Ficino's letters that he considered true friendship in this sense to be the bond that united the members of his Academy with each other and with himself, their common master, and that he liked to think of his Academy not merely as a school, but as a community of friends.

This conception of Platonic love was to exercise a strong influence on Italian and European literature throughout the sixteenth century. Many lyrical poets spoke of their love in terms that reflect Ficino's influence, as well as that of the *dolce stil nuovo* and of Petrarch, and there was a large body of treatises and lectures on love that derived much of their inspiration, directly or indirectly, from Ficino's commentary on the *Symposium*. In this literature, the concept of Platonic love was detached from the philosophical context in which it had originated with Ficino, and became more and more diluted and trivial. For this reason, the notion of Platonic love has acquired a slightly ridiculous ring for the modern reader. Yet we should try to recapture its original meaning, and remember that the true meaning of an idea is best understood in the context of the thought in which it originated and which in a sense made its formulation necessary. If we trace Platonic love back to its origin in Ficino, it may still seem a strange and remote concept, but we shall at least understand that it had a serious content, and that it was related to the central ideas of his philosophy.

The last aspect of Ficino's thought that I should like to discuss is his conception of religion and its relationship to philosophy. Ficino was a priest and a canon of Florence Cathedral, he had an adequate knowledge of Christian theology, and he even wrote an apologetic treatise on the Christian religion as well as several other theological works. There is not the slightest doubt that he intended to be orthodox, although some of his doctrines may seem to have dubious implications, and although he was once in danger of an ecclesiastical condemnation for the views on astrology and magic expressed in his work *De vita* (1489). He insisted on his Christian faith, submitted to the judgment of the Church, and was even willing to abandon the opinions of his favorite Platonist philosophers when they seemed to contradict Christian doctrine. So we are not surprised to hear him say that Christianity is the most perfect of all religions. At the same time he sees some merit in the variety of religions, and insists that any religion, however primitive, is related, at least indirectly, to the one true God. In this implicit tolerance toward other religions, Ficino comes very close to a concept of natural religion, a position that makes him a forerunner of Herbert of Cherbury, the Deists, and other advocates of a universal religion. Divine worship, he says, is almost as natural for men as neighing is for horses, or barking for dogs. The common religion of all nations, having one God for its object, is natural to the human species. This religion, which is again based on man's primary knowledge and love of God, is not shared by the animals, but is peculiar to man, a part of his dignity and excellence, and a compensation for the many defects and weaknesses of his nature.[10]

As to the relation between religion and philosophy, Ficino is convinced that true religion, that is, Christianity, and true philosophy, that is, Platonism, are in basic harmony with each other, and he is inclined to treat them as sisters, instead of trying to make one subservient to the other. He believes that it is the task of Platonic reason to confirm and support Christian faith and authority, and even considers it as his own mission, assigned to him by divine providence, to revive true philosophy for the benefit of true religion. For those who will not be guided by faith alone can be guided toward truth only through reason and the most perfect philosophy.[11]

In the light of this relationship, the continuity of the Platonic tradition assumes a new significance for Ficino. Since this tradition is thought to go back to Hermes and Zoroaster, it is as old as the religious tradition of the Hebrews, and thus the religious tradition of the Hebrews and Christians and the philosophical tradition of the Hermetics and Platonists run a parallel course in human history that goes from the early beginnings through antiquity and the Middle Ages down to the modern period.[12] It is in accordance with this view of Ficino that Augustinus Steuchus, a Catholic theologian of the sixteenth century, wrote *De perenni philosophia* (1540), a term which he coined for the Platonic tradition,[13] but which has been recently appropriated (with no better historical or philosophical credentials) for the tradition of Thomism.

The nature and quality of Ficino's teachings was such that they had to be reckoned with during his own lifetime and for a long time afterwards, even in those cases when he acted merely as a transmitter of earlier ideas. We have mentioned several examples of this influence already, yet it might be useful, in conclusion, to describe its nature more fully. As far as Florence is concerned, the beautiful capital of the Renaissance and, along with Athens and Paris, one of the main centers of Western civilization, we must recognize the fact that unlike the other great Florentine thinkers, who were poets or statesmen, artists or scientists, Ficino was the greatest Florentine philosopher and metaphysician in the proper sense of the word. He and his circle gave their imprint to a whole period of Florentine culture, and added an element to it that had been absent before, and that was to stay for several generations. Among the many Florentine scholars and writers of the late fifteenth century who show the impact of Ficino's Platonism, we find Cristoforo Landino, author of the *Camaldulensian Disputations* and of an influential commentary on Dante's *Commedia*, and Lorenzo de' Medici, who was not only a brilliant statesman but one of the best Italian poets of his century. Ficino's pupil Francesco da Diacceto carried his tradition into the first decades of the sixteenth century, and later in that century, Platonic philosophy was cultivated both at the new Florentine Academy of 1540 and at the University of Pisa. It is this Platonist climate of opinion in Florence and Pisa that accounts for some of the views and preconceptions of Galileo, as his writings clearly show. In the rest of Italy, Ficino was widely known and read. As we have seen, poets and prose writers drew on his theory of love, and theologians and philosophers upon his doctrine of immortality and some of his other ideas. We shall encounter his influence in some of the leading philosophers such as Patrizi and Bruno, and even those thinkers who opposed his views were impressed by his learning and acumen.

Ficino's influence was by no means limited to Italy. Already during his lifetime, his personal connections, as well as the diffusion of his writings, could be traced to most European countries, to Hungary, Bohemia, and Poland, to Spain, to the Low Countries and England, to France, and to Germany. His admirers included Reuchlin and Colet, Gaguin and Lefèvre d'Etaples, to mention only the most famous. During the sixteenth century, his writings were reprinted, collected, read, and quoted all over Europe. In Germany, his medical and astrological treatises were especially popular. His greatest vogue outside of Italy seems to have been in France.[14] He was copiously quoted or plagiarized by the prolific Symphorien Champier. The circle of Queen Marguerite of Navarre, and the poetic schools of Lyons and of the Pléiade, were other centers of his influence; they translated some of his writings into French, and also parts of his Latin version of Plato. We find elements of his Platonism in Bovillus and Postel, in Louis Le Roy and Bodin, and not so much in Peter Ramus, who sometimes called himself a Platonist, as in his mortal enemy Jacques Charpentier. Even in Descartes, in addition to the scholastic elements that have been so much emphasized recently, there are strong elements of Platonism (and Stoicism), which have been much less discussed, but are no less real for that.[15] Outside of France, we need only mention Erasmus and More, Fox Morcillo, Paracelsus and Cornelius Agrippa, and finally

Kepler to recognize the importance of Platonism for European thought in the sixteenth century, an importance that is closely linked with the writings, translations, and commentaries of Marsilio Ficino.

With the seventeenth century, after Galileo and Descartes, a new epoch began for European philosophy and science. The speculative cosmology of the Renaissance was no longer possible within the framework of a natural science based on experiments and mathematical formulas. The influence of Platonism persisted, however, in the metaphysics and epistemology of such great philosophers as Spinoza and Leibniz, Malebranche and Berkeley. It also gained a new life in such secondary currents as the school of Cambridge. Moreover, outside the realm of the sciences, even the cosmology of Renaissance Platonism survived in the poetry and occultism of later centuries. And since the authority of Plato himself remained a powerful force with many thinkers and writers, we still find in Kant and in Goethe several theories associated with his name and prestige that actually belong to his Florentine translator and commentator.[16] Coleridge, too, tells us in his *Biographia Literaria* that as a youth (and this was toward the end of the eighteenth century) he read Plato and Plotinus together with the commentaries and *Theologia Platonica* of the illustrious Florentine.[17]

It is only with the nineteenth century that Renaissance Platonism lost even this anonymous or pseudonymous influence. Its direct role as a spiritual force came to an end after the new school of historical and philological criticism had begun to make a rigorous (sometimes too rigorous) distinction between the genuine thought of Plato and that of his successors and commentators in late antiquity and during the Renaissance.

Yet although the ideas of Florentine Platonism have ceased to influence us in their original and literal form, we have begun to appreciate their true historical significance. Not only was Ficino's Platonism an important element in the philosophical thought of the Renaissance period; it also constitutes, for all its defects and weaknesses, one of the most important and interesting phases in the history of Platonism, a history which we are no longer prepared to trace back to Hermes and Zoroaster, but rather to Parmenides and the Pythagoreans, and which has not yet completed its course. For Platonism, if regarded not as the literal repetition of Plato's theories but as a constant adaptation and amalgamation of his basic motives according to the insight and convictions of each new thinker, will continue to be restated and revived in the future in many different ways as it has been in the past. Thus it may be considered with as much right as any other intellectual current in Western civilization to be a living tradition, and (why not?) a *philosophia perennis*.

4

Pico

Giovanni Pico della Mirandola enjoyed an unusual degree of affection and admiration during his lifetime, and during subsequent centuries, up to the present day, the fame and fascination of his name have remained undiminished. His appeal, which extended even to popular imagination, has proved far greater than that of most other scholars and thinkers of the Renaissance. His wealth and noble birth, his personal charm, his tragic life and early death, and the precocity and versatility of his talents have no doubt had their share in this unusual reputation. Yet behind the surface glamor, a study of his works reveals the solidity of his learning, the clarity and honesty of his thought, and the fertility of his basic ideas. Since he died at the age of 31, many of his more ambitious works remained unfinished or unwritten, and, above all, he was denied the opportunity to weave his various insights into the mellow pattern of a unified system. His brilliant thoughts remain fragmentary, but this does not detract from their intrinsic significance, or diminish their historical influence; it is merely a fact we ought to remember if we wish to arrive at a proper understanding of his work.

Pico is often treated as one of the chief representatives of Renaissance Platonism, and as a leading spirit of the Florentine Academy, along with, or even above, Ficino. This view is not entirely wrong, but it calls for several important qualifications. Pico spent the last and

54

most productive six years of his life in Florence, was linked by a close friendship with Ficino and other members of his circle, and probably attended many meetings of the Platonic Academy. Several members of the Academy were as much influenced by him as by Ficino. Yet the Academy had been active for twenty-six years before Pico settled in Florence, Ficino was its undisputed leader, and most of its members were imbued with his teachings and untouched by those of Pico. Moreover, although Pico considered himself a pupil of Ficino, who was his senior by thirty years, he soon developed several independent philosophical doctrines, and did not hesitate to differ from Ficino on important points of doctrine, a fact that did not impair their personal friendship. For these reasons we cannot consider Pico the leader, or a typical representative, of the Florentine Academy, even though he was in a sense a member of the Academy, and though some of us may rate his contribution higher than that of Ficino himself.

We must make similar qualifications with reference to Pico's Platonism. Pico underwent the influence of Ficino, he was well read in the ancient sources of Platonism, and he attached a certain importance to its doctrines, all of which brought him closer to the position of Ficino than to the average attitude of the professional philosophers of the time. Moreover, his influence frequently operated alongside Ficino's, with whom his name was closely associated. Yet unlike Ficino, he never claimed to revive Platonic philosophy, or to give it a predominant position over other schools of philosophy. He did not even choose to call himself a Platonist, and his major goal was to reconcile and harmonize Platonism and Aristotelianism with each other and with a number of other positions. This attitude was quite understandable, for, as we shall see, he was much better acquainted with the traditions of medieval Aristotelianism than Ficino was, and he acquired a familiarity with the sources of Jewish and Arabic thought that Ficino never possessed.

Giovanni Pico was born in Mirandola in 1463. He was a younger son in the family of the Counts of Mirandola and Concordia, who ruled as feudal lords over a small territory in northern Italy. He seems to have received his first humanistic training in Latin, and perhaps in Greek, at an early age. Being destined by his mother for a career in the Church, he was named papal protonotary at the age of 10, and began to study canon law at Bologna in 1477. Two years later, he began to study philosophy at the University of Ferrara, and from 1480 to 1482 at the University of Padua, one of the chief centers of the Aristotelian tradition. In Padua, he was a pupil of the Jewish Averroist Elia del Medigo. During this time he was in touch with humanist scholars in various places, and visited Florence repeatedly, where he met Ficino and Poliziano. He spent the following years at home and on various visits, while continuing the study of Greek. In 1484, he settled for a while in Florence, and in 1485 he visited the University of Paris, still the chief center of scholastic philosophy and theology; in 1486, he returned to Florence. After becoming involved in a curious love affair, he moved to Perugia, where he studied Hebrew and Arabic under the guidance of several Jewish teachers, and where in addition to his interest in Averroes, he became first interested in the Jewish Cabala, a medieval mystical and speculative tradition that claimed to be of ancient origin and was in fact much influenced by Neoplatonic speculations. By the end of 1486, he had composed his famous nine hundred theses, and offered to defend them in Rome during the following year in a public disputation to which he invited scholars from all parts of Europe.

The content of some of his theses aroused objections from various theologians, and Pope Innocent VIII appointed a committee to have them examined. The committee condemned seven of them as unorthodox, declared six more to be dubious, and rejected Pico's explanations. When Pico published a defense of these thirteen theses, the Pope condemned all nine hundred, although Pico had signed an act of submission. Pico decided to flee to France, where he was arrested upon the request of papal envoys in 1488. Upon the intervention of several Italian princes, he was released from prison by King Charles VIII. He returned to Italy, and was allowed by the Pope to settle in Florence, under parole as it were, and under the personal protection of Lorenzo de' Medici. There he spent the remainder of his years, except for a few short visits to Ferrara, and wrote, or began to write, his most important works, remaining in close touch not only with the circle of the Medici and the Platonic Academy, but also with Savonarola. In 1493, he was acquitted of all ecclesiastical censures and restrictions by Innocent's successor, Alexander VI. He died on November 17, 1494, the very day on which Charles VIII of France made his entry into Florence, after the expulsion of Piero de' Medici.

Pico's early death, preceded by that of Lorenzo, Ermolao Barbaro, and Poliziano, and followed a few years later by that of Ficino (who had long retired from most of his activities), marked the end of a notable epoch in the history of Florentine and Italian civilization. Pico's thought belongs entirely to that age, and it is useless to speculate how his philosophy might have developed, or how he might have fitted into the next period, if he had been granted a normal span of life.

Pico's extant writings are numerous, considering the shortness of his life, and reflect the wide range of his interests. He composed a number of Italian love sonnets, some of which have been preserved, and also a great many Latin poems, most of which are lost. A number of his letters were collected after his death by his nephew, and they may be said to represent the humanist part of his literary production, along with the famous *Oration*, which was also published after his death. To the scholastic aspect of his work we may assign the nine hundred theses, and especially the *Apologia* (1487), his defense of the thirteen theses criticized by the papal commission. Another early work is his lengthy commentary on the Platonic love poem of his friend Girolamo Benivieni (1486). To his mature philosophical writings belong the *Heptaplus* (1489), a sevenfold interpretation of the first verses of *Genesis* (1:1–27), and his *De ente et uno* (1491), published posthumously. His most extensive work is his posthumous treatise against astrology, composed in twelve books. To this we may add a few short religious and theological writings, and several fragments of a commentary on the Psalms that have been preserved in a number of scattered manuscripts. We know of a few other works that he planned to write, but have no evidence that he actually did so.

A characteristic document of Pico's historical and philosophical attitude from his earlier years in his correspondence with Ermolao Barbaro (1485), which has been rightly famous among historians of Renaissance thought. Ermolao, a distinguished Venetian humanist, was a careful student of the Greek text of Aristotle, and set himself the task of making the true Aristotle known through new translations and commentaries, a task he left unfulfilled when he died young in 1493. Ermolao's admiration for the original Aristotle was accompanied by a deep contempt for his medieval Arabic and Latin interpreters, an attitude that reminds us of Petrarch, and in a letter to Pico, he called the medieval philosophers uncultured and barbarous, not deserving to be read or studied. Pico responded with a long letter in which he praises and defends the medieval philosophers, and insists with great eloquence that what counts in the writings of philosophers is not their words or style, but their thoughts or content. Whereas Ermolao, like Petrarch and the other early humanists, despised the scholastic philosophers for their lack of elegance and classical learning, Pico is willing to recognize the solidity of their thought, and to learn from them whatever truth or insight they may have to offer.[1] The line between humanism and scholasticism is clearly drawn as the borderline between rhetoric and philosophy, and Pico, though deeply imbued with humanist learning, as Ermolao recognizes in his reply, nevertheless, throws his weight on the side of scholasticism, or at least of a synthesis that would do justice to both sides in the contest.

Ficino's attitude, though less explicit, was fundamentally similar to Pico's, for he, too, absorbed a certain amount of scholastic training, and quoted several medieval philosophers, including Averroes and Aquinas, with great respect.

This is one more reason why I do not find it appropriate to treat the Florentine Platonists merely as followers of humanism, as many Italian scholars would like to do. The Renaissance Platonists represent a new and different outlook on philosophy, to which scholasticism as well as humanism made some contributions. Pico's manifesto must have made a deep impression, and it is significant that many years after Ermolao and Pico had both died, the humanist and reformer Melanchthon, who admired Aristotle but despised scholasticism, wrote a reply to Pico's letter in which he defended Ermolao's position once more.[2]

Pico's defense of the scholastic philosophers in his letter to Ermolao was merely a special instance of a much broader historical and philosophical attitude. This attitude, rightly emphasized by Pico's interpreters, is often referred to as his syncretism. The term is taken from the syncretism of late antiquity, when, prior to the rise and victory of Christianity, the diverse religions of the many peoples who formed a part of the Roman Empire were considered compatible, and when their sundry divinities were assimilated and identified with those of the Greeks and Romans. With respect to Pico, the term refers to his belief that all known philosophical and theological schools and thinkers contained certain true and valid insights that were compatible with each other and hence deserved to be restated and defended. This was the underlying idea of his projected disputation. For the nine hundred theses, including some of those that were proposed "secundum opinionem propriam," relied on the most diverse sources: Hermes, Zoroaster, Orpheus and Pythagoras, Plato and Aristotle and all the Greek followers and commentators of both, Avicenna and Averroes along with other Arabic philosophers, Thomas Aquinas and

Duns Scotus along with several other medieval Latin thinkers, and finally the Jewish Cabalists.[3]

In using all these sources, and in explicitly assigning separate groups of theses to each of them, Pico did not wish so much to display his learning—though this may have been a factor—as to emphasize his basic conviction that each and all of these thinkers had a genuine share in philosophical truth. His notion of a universal truth in which each of the different schools and thinkers participates to some extent, constitutes an attempt to deal with the apparent contrasts and contradictions in the history of philosophy, an attempt that may be compared with the efforts made by the Neoplatonists and by Hegel. Yet Pico does not believe with the ancient eclectics that all major philosophers agree in their thoughts and merely disagree in their words. Nor does he believe with Hegel and modern perspectivists that every system of thought taken as a whole represents a particular aspect of universal truth. For Pico, in accordance with his scholastic background, truth consists in a large number of true statements, and the various philosophers participate in truth insofar as their writings contain, besides numerous errors, a number of specific statements that are recognized as true and hence must be accepted. That this was his intent we may gather from his famous *Oration*, which was actually composed as an introductory speech for his projected disputation. The entire second part of this oration was designed to justify the nature and scope of his theses, and it was therefore with good reason that he repeated it almost verbatim in his *Apologia*. He insists that he is not bound by the doctrines of any master or school, but has investigated all of them. Instead of confining himself to a single school, he has chosen what suits his thought from all of them, for each has something distinctive to contribute.[4]

Pico's syncretism may be compared with that of Ficino, who had laid the ground for it in his theory of natural religion, in his conception of the Platonic tradition and its origin in Hermes, Zoroaster, and the other early theologians, and in his emphasis on the basic harmony between Platonism and Christianity. Pico used these same notions, but made them a part of a much wider and more comprehensive synthesis by introducing two important new elements: he explicitly includes Aristotle and all his Greek, Arabic, and Latin followers; and he adds to these previously known sources the Jewish Cabalists with whom he became acquainted through his Hebrew studies, thus becoming probably the first Christian scholar to make use of Cabalistic literature. These two aspects of Pico's syncretism, his attitude toward Aristotelianism and his attitude toward Cabalism, distinguish him clearly from Ficino and other predecessors; moreover, they were not only to find further development in his own later thought, but to exert a deep influence upon the philosophy of the sixteenth century. The syncretism of the Florentine Platonists has been rightly praised by several historians as a stepping-stone toward later theories of religious and philosophical tolerance; Pico, by broadening the scope and content of that syncretism, laid the foundation for a broader tolerance.

Pico's use of Cabalism consisted not so much in accepting specific Cabalist theories as in gaining recognition for Cabalism in general. Indeed, some of the theories that he seems to have borrowed from Cabalistic authors were not necessarily of Cabalistic origin at all, such as the scheme of the three worlds, elementary, celestial, and angelic, which he uses for the first three sections of his *Heptaplus*. His chief contribution, rather, was to accept the claim made by the followers of Cabalism that their writings were based on a secret tradition that went back, at least in an oral form, to Biblical times. Cabalism thus acquires a kind of parallel authority with the Bible, similar to that held by the theology of Hermes and Zoroaster in the eyes of Ficino and Pico himself. Moreover, Pico applied to Cabalism a principle that had been used for the Old Testament by all Christian writers ever since St. Paul: that is, he tried to show that the Cabalistic tradition, no less than the Hebrew Scripture, was in basic agreement with Christian theology, and hence could be taken as a prophecy and confirmation of Christian doctrine. This was his justification for studying and citing the Cabalists, as we can see already in the second part of his *Oration*. With this argument, he laid the foundation for a whole tradition of Christian Cabalism that found its defenders in Reuchlin, Giles of Viterbo, and many other thinkers in the sixteenth century and afterwards who used the Cabala for the purposes of Christian apologetics.[5]

In Pico's own work, the Cabalistic influence is most noticeable, after the time of the nine hundred theses, in his *Heptaplus* and in his fragmentary commentary on the Psalms (which is still for the most part unpublished). In a manner which goes far beyond the medieval scheme of the four senses, Pico assigns to the text of Scripture a multiple meaning that corresponds to the various parts or sections of the universe, as we can see in the *Heptaplus*. Moreover, he uses the Cabalistic method of scriptural interpretation, which assigns numerical values to the Hebrew letters, and extracts secret meanings from the text by substituting for its words other words with comparable numerical values. I had to mention this fact to prove the extent to which Cabalistic influence appears in Pico's work; despite my respect for Pico, however, I do not defend this method as philologically sound.

The other distinctive aspect of Pico's syncretism, his tendency to assume a basic agreement between Plato and Aristotle, also remained one of his major preoccupations during the later years of his life. We know that he planned to write an extensive treatise on the agreement between Plato and Aristotle, and his friends liked to call him *Princeps Concordiae*, the prince of harmony, punning upon the name of the small town of Concordia, which was among the feudal possessions of his family. The idea that Plato and Aristotle were in basic agreement, though differing in their words and appearance, was not new with Pico. We find it expressed in Cicero, who probably took it from his teacher Antiochus of Ascalon, the originator of eclecticism within the school of Plato. We find, too, that it is attributed as a program to

Ammonius Saccas, the teacher of Plotinus, and endorsed by Boethius, who planned to translate into Latin all the writings of Plato and Aristotle. Pico was not even the latest of those who tried to defend this view. Much recent scholarship has tended to bridge the gap between Plato's dialogues and Aristotle's extant later writings by interpolating the oral teaching of Plato that was supposedly close to Aristotle, and the thought of Aristotle's lost early writings that apparently was close to Plato. In this way, the difference between the two becomes gradual rather than fundamental. If we go one step further, as many scholars have done, and assume that the ideas expressed in Plato's dialogues were not seriously held by him, the difference vanishes altogether—in many ways a convenient solution, but gained at the price, as far as Plato is concerned, of sacrificing the only tangible documents we have, the dialogues, for a mirage of doubtful hypotheses and reconstructions. No wonder many Platonic scholars are not too happy with this solution. For if we go by the extant writings, the differences between Plato and Aristotle are obvious and hard to reconcile. Hence the claim that both meant the same thing means in practice that they both meant either what Plato said or what Aristotle said.

The Renaissance thinkers with whom we are concerned did not escape this dilemma. Ficino, who was not prejudiced against Aristotle, followed on the whole the Neoplatonic line: Aristotle is useful for his contributions to logic and natural philosophy, but far inferior to Plato in metaphysics and theology. Hence we must subordinate Aristotle to Plato, and follow the latter in all those cases where they seem to disagree. Pico, thanks to his thorough scholastic training, had a much stronger allegiance to Aristotle and his school. If Plotinus and other Neoplatonists understood Plato in a way that contradicted Aristotle, they must be wrong both in their philosophical opinions and in their understanding of Plato.

This is roughly Pico's approach in *De ente et uno,* a little treatise composed toward the end of his life and the only surviving fragment, perhaps all that was ever written, of his projected work on the harmony between Plato and Aristotle. The issue is interesting and historically important. The question is whether being and unity are coextensive, as Aristotle maintains in the tenth book of his *Metaphysics,* or whether unity has a broader diffusion than being, since it originates in a higher metaphysical principle, according to the view of Plotinus and other Neoplatonists. Following the scholastic doctrine of the transcendentals, Pico sets out to defend the position of Aristotle. He then tries to prove that Plato did not hold the opposite view, as claimed by the Neoplatonists. In support of his claim, Pico cites a passage from Plato's *Sophist,* and dismisses the testimony of the *Parmenides,* arguing that this dialogue is merely a dialectical exercise. (In this view, Pico receives the support of a recent scholar,[6] but runs counter to the opinion of Hegel, who considered the *Parmenides* the most speculative of Plato's writings.)

We cannot follow all of Pico's arguments on this complicated subject, but we may call attention to his acute distinction between being itself and participated being, which makes it possible for him to maintain that God is identical with being in the former sense, but above being in the latter.[7] The harmony between Plato and Aristotle turns out to be quite Aristotelian, at least in its wording, since it excludes the views of Plotinus and the Neoplatonists; but in another sense it is neither Platonic nor Aristotelian. As a result, Pico's position was criticized on the one side by Ficino, who defended Plotinus in his commentary on the *Parmenides,* and on the other by the Aristotelian Antonio Cittadini, who formulated a series of objections that were answered first by Pico himself, and then by his nephew and editor Gianfrancesco Pico.[8] This three-cornered controversy throws an interesting light on the interpretation and influence of Plato, Aristotle, and Plotinus during this period, and deserves closer study than it has received so far.

Another aspect of Pico's thought, which we might relate to his syncretism, consists in his treatment of classical mythology. An allegorical interpretation of the myths of the Greek poets had been developed by the ancient philosophers, especially by the Stoics and Neoplatonists, and for them it had been a device for reconciling pagan religion with philosophical truth. When the medieval grammarians continued to interpret the classical poets in this manner, they minimized the pagan religious element and emphasized the implied universal, or even Christian, truth that would justify the study of these writers. The method was taken over and further developed by the humanists, and we find notable examples of it in Salutati's treatment of the labors of Hercules (before 1406),[9] and in Landino's *Camaldulensian Disputationes* (ca. 1475), which contain an elaborate moral exegesis of the plot of Vergil's *Aeneid*. Ficino continued the tradition, drawing not merely on these immediate precedents, but also on his Neoplatonic authorities, when he embroidered his writings with accounts and allegorical explanations of ancient myths. His commentary on Plato's *Symposium* is full of such passages, as are his letters. A noteworthy example is his treatment of the judgment of Paris in an appendix to his commentary on Plato's *Philebus*.[10] Pico tends to be even more elaborate in his discussion and interpretation of ancient myths, especially in his commentary on Benivieni's love poem, which in a sense belongs to the same genre and tradition as Ficino's commentary on the *Symposium*. It is in this work that Pico repeatedly mentions his plan to write a treatise on poetic theology. No fragments of this work have come down to us, and he may never have carried out his plan. But in line with Aristotle's view that the poets were the first theologians, it seems to have been Pico's intention to construct a detailed system of the theology implicit in the myths of the ancient poets.[11] In this way, he would have illustrated their share in the common truth, and thus have included them in the universal syncretism that comprised all philosophers and theologians known to him.

Much more famous than the ideas so far discussed is Pico's doctrine of the dignity of man and his place in the universe. The oration in which this doctrine is developed constitutes perhaps the most widely known document of early Renaissance thought. In many editions the work is entitled *Oration on the Dignity of Man,* but, as many scholars have observed, this title properly belongs only to the first part of the oration. The original title of the work was simply *Oration.* It was composed as an opening speech for the projected disputation, and, as we have noted, the second part (which does not deal with the theme of human dignity) contains the actual program of the disputation, and therefore would have been especially appropriate for the occasion for which it was written. The words "on the Dignity of Man" were simply added to the title at a later date because people were particularly impressed with the idea that dominated the first part of the speech, perhaps not even reading beyond it to the end, as often happens with hasty readers.

The emphasis on man and his dignity is implicit in the very program of the *studia humanitatis,* as we have seen, and hence the subject is often referred to by the humanists, down to Facio and Manetti, who dedicated entire treatises to it. It has been shown, and even appears from their quotations, that the humanists drew for their specific arguments on ancient and patristic, if not on medieval, sources when dealing with this theme. We have also seen that the topic was taken up by Ficino, and received a kind of metaphysical framework from him, when he assigned to the human soul a privileged place in the center of the universal hierarchy, and made it, both through its intermediary attributes and through its universal thought and aspirations, the bond of the universe and the link between the intelligible and the corporeal world.

In his *Oration,* Pico went beyond Ficino in several ways. Most important, he did not discuss the question merely in passing, or within the context of a large work dedicated to other subjects, but displayed it prominently in the opening section of a short and elegantly written oration. Moreover, he lays the accent not so much on man's universality as on his freedom: instead of assigning to him a fixed, though privileged, place in the universal hierarchy, he puts him entirely apart from this hierarchy, and claims that he is capable of occupying, according to his choice, any degree of life from the lowest to the highest. Neither a fixed abode, so he has God address Adam, nor a form that is thine alone, nor any function peculiar to thyself have we given thee, Adam, to the end that according to thy judgment thou mayest have and possess what abode, what form, and what functions thou thyself shalt desire. Constrained by no limits, in accordance with thine own free will, in whose hand we have placed thee, thou shalt ordain for thyself the limits of thy nature. Thou shalt have the power to degenerate into the lower forms of life, which are brutish. Thou shalt have the power, out of thy soul's judgment, to be reborn into the higher forms, which are divine.[12]

These words have a modern ring, and they are among the few passages in the philosophical literature of the Renaissance that have pleased, almost without reservation, modern, and even existentialist, ears. I am not absolutely sure they were meant to be as modern as they sound, and I hardly believe, what has often been said, that when Pico wrote them he had denied or forgotten the doctrine of grace. After all, the words are attributed to God, and addressed by Him to Adam before the Fall. Yet they do contain an eloquent praise of human excellence and man's potentialities, and they receive added vigor when we think of what the reformers, and even great humanists like Montaigne, were to say about man's vanity and weakness.

Some scholars have tried to minimize Pico's praise of human dignity, and regard it as a mere piece of oratory. This view is refuted by the testimony of the *Heptaplus,* a work written several years later and for an entirely different purpose. Here again Pico places man outside the hierarchy of the three worlds, the angelic, celestial, and elementary, treats him as a fourth world by himself, and praises him and his faculties, although within a more obvious theological context.[13]

Pico's insistence on man's dignity and liberty also accounts, at least in part, for his attack on astrology, to which he dedicates his longest extant work, probably composed during the last few years of his life. This work is full of detailed astronomical discussions, which we cannot describe here, and displays an amazing mastery of the astrological and anti-astrological literature of previous centuries. It has often been hailed by modern historians as a landmark in the struggle of science against superstition. In fact, Pico does state that the stars act upon sublunar things only through their light and heat, not through any other occult qualities that may be attributed to them,[14] and this statement sounds very sober, if not necessarily modern. Moreover, we learn that no less a scientist than Kepler at least modified his initial belief in astrology under the impression of Pico's treatise.[15] Yet in Pico's time the belief in astrology was more than a superstition, and the rejection of it was not necessarily scientific. As a general system, astrology was closely linked with the scientific cosmology of the age, and hence widely accepted, not only by quacks, but also by serious thinkers including Pontano, Ficino, and Pomponazzi. There is no evidence that Pico was especially guided by scientific considerations in this respect, and we must face the fact that he accepted natural magic while rejecting astrology. We happen to know that his work against astrology was composed as a part of a larger work he planned to write, and left unfinished at the time of his death, and that this work was to be directed against the enemies of the Church. The basic impulse of his attack was religious and not scientific, and he indicates more than once what his chief objection to astrology was: the stars are bodies, and ourselves are spirits; it cannot be admitted that a corporeal, and hence lower, being should act upon our higher self and restrict its freedom.[16]

Let us finally say a word about Pico's conception of the relation between philosophy and religion. It is quite evident from a number of documents that Pico became increasingly concerned with religious problems during his later years, a development in which his shock at the papal condemnation of his theses and the influence of Savonarola must have played a part. The fact appears in the religious and theological content of several of his later writings, as well as in the religious motivation of his treatise against astrology. It also finds an unexpected expression in certain passages of the *De ente et uno,* a work that deals fundamentally with a very different problem. Here Pico tells us that God is darkness, and that philosophical knowledge can lead us toward God only up to a certain point, beyond which religion must guide us.[17] At least at this stage of his thought, Pico is more "mystical" than Ficino, who carries the parallelism of philosophy and religion to its ultimate extreme, and for whom there is no limit to philosophical knowledge. For Pico, by contrast, religion seems to be a fulfillment of philosophy: religion helps us to attain that ultimate end for which philosophy can merely prepare us.[18]

I hope to have shown that Pico's ideas were quite significant and independent, although he did not live long enough to work them out into a coherent whole. Fragmentary as it was, his work had wide repercussions for a long time. His syncretism was more comprehensive than that of Ficino, and therefore came closer to subsequent efforts at formulating a universal religion. His study of Hebrew and Arabic, although not entirely without precedents, served as a widely known example and gave a powerful impulse to these studies in Christian Europe, leading to a study of the Hebrew Scripture and to many new translations of Jewish and Arabic texts. His study and use of the Cabala started a broad and powerful current of Christian Cabalism, which flourished throughout the sixteenth century and counted among its representatives many distinguished scholars and thinkers. In the eyes of many scholars of the later Renaissance, the Cabalistic literature so highly praised by Pico joined the company of Plato and the Neoplatonists, of Hermes, Zoroaster, Orpheus, and the other pagan theologians who had received their credentials from Ficino ("ille mirabilis sciendi ac nesciendi auctor," as he was to be called by a nineteenth-century scholar[19]). Here was a large body of philosophical and metaphysical literature that was not of Christian origin, but believed to be in basic harmony with the teachings of Christianity, a literature that was in part profound, in part given an appearance of depth by honest belief and laborious interpretation—a literature quite different from that of the Aristotelian tradition, which might or might not be reconciled with that tradition, but which in any case constituted the most compact body of philosophical ideas that was available besides it.

This was perhaps the strangest part of the complex inheritance that Florentine Platonism—Ficino and Pico together—left to the philosophy, theology, and literature of the sixteenth century, and to its later successors—philosophers, poets, and occultists—down to the time of Romanticism, and even down to our own time. Part of this heritage is distasteful to some of us, including myself, while other parts are admirable and impressive. We must resign ourselves to the fact that in the thought of the past, as perhaps in that of our own time, truth and error, sense and nonsense, are combined and interwoven. As historians we must accept the mixture as it is offered to us by the sources of the past. As philosophers, the best we can do is to practice upon Pico and his companions and followers what he tried to do with his predecessors: to take from them whatever truth and sense they were able to express, and to respect and even admire them for whatever share they had in the universal truth that will always be discovered only in parts. In Pico's case, we should give him credit for having raised his axe, though not for scientific reasons, against a superstition, astrology, that was to remain respectable for another hundred years or more until scientists greater than he managed to put an end to its respectability (though not its life). Finally, Pico's song of the dignity of man has been heard over the centuries up to our own time, even by those who have been deaf to the rest of the concert of Renaissance thought, even by the self-styled modern humanists who have forgotten that *humanitas* includes, besides friendly feelings, a liberal education and some learning (I hardly dare to call this notion vulgar, as Gellius once did[20]). Let it be enough to remember that in praising man and his dignity, Pico was summing up the aspiration of several generations of learned humanists, adding to it something of which they were not capable, namely, a metaphysical context and a philosophical meaning.

5

Pomponazzi

Pomponazzi belonged to the same generation as Pico, but with his work we enter a new century, the sixteenth, and a different school of philosophy, Aristotelianism. We should not call it a new school, for its ancient origins were about as old as those of Platonism, and its medieval antecedents far more continuous and more firmly rooted in institutional traditions, at least after the twelfth century. If we date humanism from its rise in Italy toward the end of the thirteenth century, Aristotelianism is the slightly older school, though at least in Italy not by very much. The coexistence of, and occasional rivalry between, humanism and Aristotelianism is best understood if we realize that humanism was professionally and academically associated with the *studia humanitatis,* and Aristotelianism with the philosophical disciplines, especially logic, natural philosophy, and, to a lesser extent, metaphysics; moral philosophy alone was claimed by the humanists as a part of their domain. We may compare the rivalry between the two traditions, with some appropriate qualifications, to the modern rivalry between the sciences and the humanities.

The rise of Aristotelianism in the twelfth and thirteenth centuries was one of the major events in the intellectual history of the Middle Ages. It reflected, first, the expansion of learning beyond the narrow limits of the seven liberal arts that had encompassed the horizon of the earlier medieval centuries; second, the introduction, through Latin

72

translations from the Greek and Arabic, of a vast body of scientific and philosophical literature previously unavailable to Western readers, in which the works of Aristotle and his Arabic commentator Averroes played an especially important role; and, third, the emergence, especially in France, England, and Italy, of new institutions of higher learning, the universities, where the advanced disciplines including philosophy, now emancipated from the encyclopedia of the liberal arts, were taught by and for specialists, on the basis of the newly acquired texts and with a newly developed method. This method involved the use of the class lecture and the disputation, which found their literary expression in the commentary and the question, and the adoption of standard authorities, a fixed technical terminology, and a highly developed and strictly regulated method of reasoning and of formulating arguments.

At the University of Paris and other Northern universities, the texts of Aristotle and the commentaries of Averroes became firmly established, after some initial resistance, by the middle of the thirteenth century. Philosophy, therefore, was, and always remained, distinct from theology, although, owing to the dominating position of theology at these universities, it was often studied and taught as a preparation for theology. In Italy the role of Aristotelianism developed in a quite different way. At the Italian universities, throughout the medieval and Renaissance period, theology was either absent, or played a marginal and subordinate role. These universities originated as schools of medicine and law, and when the study of Aristotelian philosophy was introduced, it came to be closely associated with that of medicine.

The earliest traces of this tendency may be seen at Salerno during the second half of the twelfth century, but its full development began at Bologna during the second half of the thirteenth century, and spread from there to Padua and other universities. From the end of the thirteenth century on—that is, about the same time as the rise of Italian humanism—the Italian universities produced a steady and continuous

73

sequence of teachers of Aristotelian philosophy, and a voluminous literature which grew out of their teaching, and which is still largely unexplored. The Italian Aristotelian tradition continued to flourish vigorously throughout the fifteenth and sixteenth centuries and lasted even into the seventeenth. It is therefore hard to believe those literary historians who claim that Aristotelianism was defeated by Petrarch and his humanist followers; for it produced some of its most important representatives long after the time of Petrarch.

This tradition must be called Aristotelian on account of its sources and authorities, and also scholastic on account of its terminology, method, and style. Yet it was thoroughly secular, and, if you wish, naturalistic, because of its close ties with medicine and its lack of connection with theology (though it was not opposed to theology, let alone to religion, as has often been claimed). It is frequently referred to as Averroism, but I should prefer to call it secular Aristotelianism; for the use of Averroes' commentary was not peculiar to this school, nor were the distinctive theories of Averroes, such as the unity of the intellect, consistently accepted by the Italian Aristotelians. It is also often referred to as the school of Padua, but I prefer to call it the Italian school. The University of Padua came to occupy an especially important place in the Aristotelian tradition during the fifteenth and sixteenth centuries, but it had no monopoly in the movement, nor was there any uniformity about its teaching. Moreover, during the earlier period up to the middle of the fourteenth century, Padua was less important than Bologna in this development, and even after that date the contribution of other universities was much greater than is commonly known.

It is this tradition of Italian Aristotelianism, usually called Paduan Averroism, that produced Pomponazzi, and along with him a whole line of distinguished Aristotelian philosophers whom we shall have no occasion to mention. Pomponazzi must stand for us as a representative of a broad philosophical movement which is often forgotten by historians of the Italian Renaissance, but which actually accounts for a large part of the academic and literary activity of the period in the field of philosophy. As one of its most distinguished representatives, Pomponazzi bears witness to the significance and vitality of that movement.

By Pomponazzi's time, Italian Aristotelianism had been flourishing for several centuries, had survived the attacks of Petrarch and other humanists, and had received important new impulses from Paris and Oxford toward the end of the fourteenth century.

There is no doubt that Pomponazzi, on account of his training and career, his sources and authorities, his method and style, must be considered as a typical product of this school. However, it would be wrong to assume that he was completely untouched by the other currents of his time, or to be surprised because a simple label like Aristotelianism, in his case as in so many others, proves inadequate to describe the complex thought of an original and vigorous thinker. Pomponazzi read and respected the writings of Ficino, to whom he owed his acquaintance with Plato and perhaps his preoccupation with the problem of immortality. The way in which he speaks about the position of man in the universe is clearly influenced by both Ficino and Pico. He also shows at many other points the impact of the broad humanist movement of his time. He cultivates the monographic treatise, in addition to the commentary and question, and even makes a timid attempt to use the form of the dialogue. He occasionally likes to speak of himself in good humanist fashion, and cites such favorite humanist sources as Cicero and Plutarch. His doctrine that virtue is its own reward has Stoic rather than Aristotelian antecedents, and his insistence that the end of man consists in practical virtue rather than contemplation is at variance with Aristotle, and may owe something to Cicero and the civic humanism of such earlier humanists as Bruni and Alberti.

We may even link with the humanist tradition Pomponazzi's interest in Alexander of Aphrodisias, the Greek commentator of Aristotle, who was not entirely unknown during the Middle Ages, but whose writings acquired a much wider diffusion through new translations around the turn of the sixteenth century.[1] Although the label of Alexandrism, often attached to Pomponazzi, is quite dubious and misleading, we know from an early question composed by Pomponazzi in 1504 that his view on the problem of immortality, as adopted in his later treatise of 1516, was derived from that of Alexander. We also learn that his treatise *De fato* was occasioned by reading a new translation of Alexander's treatise on the subject, although it turns out that the work of the so-called Alexandrist Pomponazzi is actually a defense of the Stoic position against Alexander. I hope these preliminary remarks have not caused too great a confusion, but have helped to dispel some of the wrong and misleading notions with which the name of Pomponazzi is often associated.

Pietro Pomponazzi was born in Mantua in 1462. He studied philosophy at the University of Padua, and after obtaining his degree, he became extraordinary professor of philosophy in 1488 and ordinary or full professor in 1495. When the university was closed as a result of the war of the League of Cambrai in 1509, he left Padua, stayed for a while with Alberto Pio, lord of Carpi, then moved to the University of Ferrara, and finally accepted a professorship at the University of Bologna, where he taught from 1512 until his death in 1525. He married three times and had two children.

Of Pomponazzi's writings, only a few were published during his lifetime. Best known is the treatise "On the Immortality of the Soul" (*De immortalitate animae,* 1516), which immediately provoked a great controversy, was publicly attacked by several philosophers and theologians, and was followed up by the author with two defensive treatises that were longer than the original work itself. Probably as a result of this experience, Pomponazzi did not publish anything else, except for a few short philosophical questions of a non-controversial nature that he added to the 1525 reprint of his three writings on immortality. Equally important are his treatises *De incantationibus* and *De fato,* both composed around 1520, which were published post-humously in Basel by a Protestant exile in 1556 and 1567, respectively. A sizable body of other writings has been preserved in manuscript, and the study and publication of this material has barely been started. The more important among these unpublished writings are questions on Aristotelian and other problems, which he probably worded himself, and which therefore reflect his thought quite directly. Another large group consists of his class lectures on various works of Aristotle. Since they were taken down by students and show a certain amount of oscil-lation from year to year, and from copy to copy, they must be used with caution in any attempt to reconstruct Pomponazzi's thought and philosophical development.

Pomponazzi's style is as far removed from humanist elegance as it can be, and represents a rather harsh example of scholastic terminology and argument, although he is at times capable of concise formulation and caustic wit. His reasoning shows great subtlety and acumen, but he is repetitious and sometimes inconsistent. He obviously enjoys spin-ning out an argument and following reason wherever it leads, and out of intellectual honesty, he is prepared to admit his puzzlement in front of certain dilemmas, or to modify his views whenever he feels com-pelled to do so by some strong argument. Thus we may well under-stand his famous outburst in the third book of the *De fato* (ch. 7), where he cites the mythical Prometheus as a prototype of the philoso-pher who, in the course of his efforts to understand the secrets of God, is eaten up by his continuous worries and thoughts, stops eating, drink-ing, and sleeping, is held up to ridicule by all, taken as a fool and a faithless person, persecuted by the Inquisition, and laughed at by the multitude.[2]

The *De incantationibus* is an attempt to offer all kinds of natural explanations for a number of occurrences popularly ascribed to the agency of demons and spirits. It is significant that for Pomponazzi the effects ascribed to the stars by the astrologers form a part of the system of natural causes. This work is the only one by Pomponazzi that was once on the index of prohibited books (it no longer is), on account of its implied criticism of miracles. It contains an interesting passage on prayer, which shows a certain affinity with some of the ideas expressed in the treatise on immortality. The value of prayer, he says, consists not in the external effects it may have, but in the pious attitude it produces in the person who prays.[3]

In the *De fato*, which is divided into five books and is by far the longest of his works, Pomponazzi discusses in great detail, and with a great number of intricate arguments, the problems of fate, free will, and predestination. His conclusions are by no means simple or clear-cut, but it appears from his final conclusion that he regards the Stoic doctrine of fate, on purely natural grounds, as relatively free from contradictions. Yet since human wisdom is subject to error, he is willing to submit to the teaching of the Church, and to accept the doctrine that God's providence and predestination are compatible with man's free will. However, he is not satisfied with the way in which this compatibility is customarily explained, and tries instead to propose an explanation that he considers more satisfactory.[4]

We cannot go into further detail concerning this important work. It has been unduly neglected even by students of Pomponazzi, perhaps on account of its length and difficulty. It is now available in a critical edition, and hopefully it will some day be studied within the twofold historical context in which it belongs: that is, the philosophical controversy between determinism and indeterminism, as it appeared in antiquity in the works of the Stoics and Alexander, and again in more modern discussions; and the specifically theological problem of reconciling providence and predestination with free will. This last question has occupied Christian theologians of all centuries; we have encountered it in Valla's treatise on free will, and it was to be debated by Luther and Erasmus, and by many other theologians during and after the Reformation.

I should like to discuss at greater length Pomponazzi's treatise on immortality, which is much better known, and which had far wider repercussions during the sixteenth century and even later. Pomponazzi explains the origin of the treatise as follows: he had stated in a class lecture that Thomas Aquinas's view on immortality, though perhaps true, did not agree with Aristotle's, and he was subsequently asked by a Dominican friar who was his student to express his own opinion on the question, staying strictly within the limits of natural reason.[5]

In complying with this request, Pomponazzi begins with the statement that man is of a manifold and ambiguous nature, and occupies an intermediary position between mortal and immortal things (ch. 1). The question is in what sense such contrary attributes as mortal and immortal may be attributed to the human soul (ch. 2).

Pomponazzi first lists six possible answers, and after having discarded two of them, because they have never been defended by anybody, he promises to discuss the remaining four (chs. 2–3).

The first of these four is the view attributed to Averroes and others, according to which there is only one immortal soul common to all human beings, and also an individual soul for each person, which, however, is mortal. In Chapter 4 of his treatise, Pomponazzi rejects this opinion at great length. The Averroist position maintains that the intellect is capable of acting without a body, and can therefore be regarded as separable and immortal. Yet in our experience, Pomponazzi argues, the intellect has no action that is entirely independent of the body, and therefore we have no evidence that the intellect is separable. If we wish to understand the relationship of the intellect to the body, we must distinguish between being in the body as having the body for its organ or subject or substratum, and depending on the body as having the body, its perceptions, and imaginations for its object. Pomponazzi insists that the intellect does not use the body as its subject, as is the case for the souls of the animals and for the lower faculties of the human soul. Yet the human intellect cannot know anything without perceptions or imaginations offered to it by the body, and this fact alone proves that the intellect is not separable from the body.[6]

Second, Pomponazzi discusses an opinion that he attributes to Plato, according to which each individual person has two different souls, one immortal and the other mortal (ch. 5). This position is rejected on the ground that the subject of perception and that of intellectual knowledge must be one and the same, and that it is therefore not possible to distinguish two separate natures within the same human soul (ch. 6).

Third, he examines the view attributed to Thomas Aquinas, which holds that the human soul has but a single nature, and that it is absolutely (*simpliciter*) immortal, and only in some respects (*secundum quid*) mortal (ch. 7). Elaborating on some of the arguments he had already advanced against Averroes, Pomponazzi insists that he finds no evidence to prove the absolute immortality of the soul. He has no doubt, he adds, that the doctrine of the absolute immortality of the soul is true, since it is in accordance with Scripture, but he wonders whether it is in agreement with Aristotle, and whether it can be established within the limits of natural reason without recurring to the evidence of faith and revelation (ch. 8).[7]

Fourth and last, Pomponazzi discusses a position according to which the human soul, having only one nature, is absolutely mortal, and only in certain respects immortal (ch. 9). He then proceeds to defend this position, which he had identified elsewhere as that of Alexander of Aphrodisias. Insisting once more on the middle position of man, he argues that the human intellect, unlike that of the pure intelligences, always needs the body for its object and has no way of acting without the help of sense images. It must therefore be considered absolutely mortal. On the other hand, unlike the souls of the animals, the human intellect does not use the body as its subject. Therefore, it may be said to participate in immortality, or to be immortal in some respects. This position is claimed to be more probable than the others, and to be more in accordance with the teachings of Aristotle (chs. 9–10).

Having reached this conclusion in Chapter 10, Pomponazzi continues in good scholastic fashion to formulate several sets of objections to this view (chs. 11 and 13), and to answer these objections one by one in great detail (chs. 12 and 14). In the course of the discussion, he repeats and elaborates some of the arguments presented in the preceding chapters. He also introduces new arguments and conclusions, especially in Chapter 14, which are of great intrinsic interest, and which we must discuss a little further.

Yet it might be best to report first his final conclusion as set forth in the last chapter. Having presented all arguments against the immortality of the soul, Pomponazzi states that the question is a neutral one, as is the eternity of the world. In other words, he does not believe that there are any natural reasons strong enough to demonstrate the immortality of the soul, or to refute its mortality, although he knows that many theologians, notably Thomas Aquinas, have argued otherwise. Since the question is thus doubtful on purely human grounds, it must be resolved by God Himself, Who clearly proved the immortality of the soul in the Holy Scriptures. This means that the arguments to the contrary must be false and merely apparent. The immortality of the soul is an article of faith, for it is based on faith and revelation. Hence it must be asserted on this ground alone, and not on the basis of inconclusive or unconvincing rational arguments.[8]

Before taking leave of this treatise, let us return to some of the important ideas formulated in Chapter 14 as a reply to certain objections, and also try to interpret the meaning of Pomponazzi's conclusion, which has been the subject of much debate among historians of philosophy.

Along with other objections to his view, Pomponazzi cites in Chapter 13 the argument that according to Aristotle's *Ethics* the ultimate end of man is contemplation, and that the satisfactory fulfillment of this end requires immortality.[9] In his reply, he states that man has a threefold intellect: speculative, practical, and technical. Only a few persons have a share in the speculative intellect, whereas the technical intellect is shared by some animals. Thus we may conclude that the practical intellect, in which all human beings, and only all human beings, share, is the faculty peculiar to human beings. Every normal person can attain the practical intellect in a perfect way, and a person is called absolutely good or bad with reference to this practical intellect, but merely in some respect good or bad with reference to the other two intellects. For a man is called a good man or a bad man with reference to his virtues and vices, yet a good metaphysician with reference to his speculative intellect, and a good architect with reference to his technical intellect. However, a good metaphysician or a good architect is not always a good man. Hence a man does not mind so much if he is not called a good metaphysician or a good architect, but he minds very much if he is called unjust or intemperate. For it seems to be in our power to be good or wicked, but to be a philosopher or an architect does not depend on us, and is not necessary for a man. Hence the ultimate end must be defined in terms of the practical intellect, and every man is called upon to be as virtuous as possible. By contrast, it is neither necessary nor even desirable that all men should be philosophers or architects, but only that some of them should be. Moreover, since the perfection of the practical intellect is accessible to almost everybody, a farmer or a craftsman, a poor man or a rich man, may be called happy, and actually is called happy, and is satisfied with his lot, whenever he is virtuous. In other words, Pomponazzi departs in this important respect from Aristotle, and identifies the end of human life with moral virtue, rather than with contemplation, because this end is attainable by all human beings without exception.[10]

There had been another objection that God would not be a good governor of all things unless all good deeds found their reward, and all bad deeds their punishment, in a future life. To this Pomponazzi replies that the essential reward of virtue is virtue itself, and the essential punishment of vice, vice itself. Hence it makes no difference whether the external or accidental reward or punishment of an action is sometimes omitted, since its essential reward and punishment are always present. Moreover, if one man acts virtuously without the expectation of a reward, and another with such an expectation, the act of the latter is not considered to be so virtuous as that of the former. Thus he who receives no external reward is rewarded more fully in an essential way than he who receives one. In the same way, the wicked person who receives no external punishment is punished worse than he who does. For the punishment inherent in guilt itself is much worse than any punishment in the form of some harm or damage inflicted upon the guilty person.[11]

Pomponazzi further develops this idea in reply to another objection. It is true that religious teachers have supported the doctrine of immortality, but they have done so in order to induce ordinary people to lead a virtuous life. Yet persons of a higher moral disposition are attracted toward the virtues by the mere excellence of these virtues, and are repelled from the vices by the mere ugliness of these vices, and hence do not need the expectation of rewards or punishments as an incentive. Rejecting the view that without a belief in immortality no moral standards could be maintained, Pomponazzi repeats that a virtuous action without the expectation of a reward is superior to one that aims at a reward, and concludes that those who assert that the soul is mortal seem to preserve the notion of virtue much better than those who assert that it is immortal.[12]

In other words, drawing on certain passages in Plato, and above all on the doctrine of the Stoics, Pomponazzi strongly expresses his conviction that virtue is its own reward, and vice its own punishment. In thus stating that moral standards, as defined by the philosopher, do not depend on religious sanctions, he does not deny the validity of religious beliefs, but asserts the autonomy of reason and philosophy, anticipating to some extent the views of Spinoza and Kant. His views seem to me far superior to those contrary opinions that are often expressed and propagated even in our days, and that usually go unchallenged.

The last point brings us to a problem that concerns the final conclusion of Pomponazzi's treatise, and also the conclusion of his *De fato*. The statement made by many theological contemporaries of Pomponazzi, and by some modern historians, that he simply denied the immortality of the soul is obviously false. He merely says that the immortality of the soul cannot be demonstrated on purely natural grounds, or in accordance with Aristotle, but must be accepted as an article of faith. This position is widely, and somewhat crudely, referred to as the theory of the double truth. The term is inadequate, for neither Pomponazzi nor anybody else ever said that something is true in theology, and its very opposite true in philosophy. What Pomponazzi did say, and what many respectable thinkers said before and after him, is that one theory—for example, that of the immortality of the soul— is true according to faith, but that it cannot be demonstrated on the basis of mere reason, and that its opposite would seem to be supported by equally strong or even stronger probable arguments.

This view has been called absurd by many modern historians, and ironically by some who actually take a similar position themselves, though perhaps on other issues and with different words, holding some ideas, such as creation, to be true in one context, and at least indemonstrable in another. Yet the persistent charge made against Pomponazzi, and against many other medieval and Renaissance thinkers who took a similar position, has been that the so-called theory of the double truth is merely a hypocritical device to disguise their secret disbelief and avoid trouble with the Church authorities. Thus in saying that immortality cannot be demonstrated, and that mortality may be defended by strong rational arguments whereas immortality is to be held as an article of faith, Pomponazzi, according to these historians, merely concealed his opinion that the soul was really mortal, and substituted for it a formula that would protect him against ecclesiastic censure or punishment.

The problem is as serious as it is delicate. We certainly are in no position to deny that a thinker of the past may have entertained thoughts and opinions which for one reason or another did not find expression in his writings, or that he may have put into writing views which he may not have seriously maintained in his innermost heart. This admission is quite legitimate as a counsel of modesty on the part of the historian, but it hardly entitles us to go one step further and assert in a positive way that a thinker held some specific views which he failed to express in his writings, or which are even in contrast with his expressed views. As a theologian of the eighteenth century said on this very matter, we must leave it to God to look into Pomponazzi's heart and to see what his real opinion was. The human historian has no other basis but the written document, and the burden of proof, in history as before the law, rests with him who wants to prove something that is contrary to the overt evidence. Neither innuendo nor the assertions made by unfriendly critics or extremist followers can be accepted as valid evidence in lieu of some original statement or testimony concerning the author's view.

According to this standard, we have no real grounds for maintaining that Pomponazzi was hypocritical. The position he takes in the treatise on the immortality of the soul is fundamentally retained in two lengthy works he composed afterwards in defense of the first treatise, and, with a few dubious exceptions, also in his questions and class lectures. He was attacked by some theologians, but defended by others, and his treatise was not condemned by the Church authorities. The general view that immortality could not be rationally demonstrated, if not all the specific opinions that Pomponazzi associated with it, was held also by Duns Scotus, and even by the leading Thomist of Pomponazzi's time, Cardinal Cajetan. After the first excitement had passed, Pomponazzi continued to teach at a university located within the papal states, had many clergymen among his students who apparently found no offense in what he said, and died peacefully as a widely respected scholar. The pupil who took his remains to his home town and erected a monument for him was Ercole Gonzaga, a later cardinal and president of the Council of Trent. If there is any presumptive evidence, it hardly favors the opinion that Pomponazzi was a secret disbeliever or atheist.

Speaking more broadly, we may say that the so-called theory of the double truth is not satisfactory in a purely logical sense. Nevertheless, it is at least an apparent solution of a dilemma for those who perceive a conflict between faith and reason, and wish to hold on to both. For those who can dispense ·with one or the other, the conflict ceases to exist, and the solution becomes superfluous. In the case of Pomponazzi, as in that of many other thinkers, the theory makes perfect sense, if we do not take it as a hypocritical attack upon faith, but as a sincere attempt to defend the coexistence of faith and reason, or of theology and philosophy, and to emphasize the relative independence of reason and philosophy within their own domain. In this sense, the position must appear to retain some of its validity even at the present time.

If we compare Pomponazzi's position with that of Ficino, and focus our attention on the problem of immortality, which was central for both of them, the contrast is significant and instructive. In a way, both thinkers are rationalists. Yet Ficino bases his postulate of immortality on the appeal to an inner experience and knowledge that is independent of all corporeal influences, and that gives us evidence, even during the present life, of an incorporeal reality. In this he follows the Platonic tradition. Pomponazzi, on the other hand, denies the possibility of any human knowledge that would be completely independent of corporeal data, and it is for this reason that he can see no basis, on purely natural grounds, for assuming that our intellect is separable or immortal. In this sense, Pomponazzi is a more radical empiricist than Averroes, and perhaps than Aristotle himself, and it is no coincidence that he falls back on Alexander of Aphrodisias, the most naturalistic and least Platonic of all commentators of Aristotle.

Moreover, Ficino saw the dignity of man and the ultimate end of his existence in the contemplative life, and was driven to postulate the immortality of the soul in order to make this end attainable for a larger number of persons. Pomponazzi, by contrast, placed the ultimate end of life in moral action, which is attainable by most people during the present life, whereas contemplation is not. Since for him virtue is its own reward, no future reward is needed for its fulfillment, and the dignity of man can be realized during the present life.

Ficino believed in the basic harmony between reason, that is, Platonic reason, and Christian faith, and was convinced that the immortality of the soul and the other basic teachings of religion could be demonstrated or confirmed by philosophical argument. Pomponazzi saw a basic disagreement between natural or Aristotelian reason and Christian doctrine. He merely tried to follow reason and its arguments as far as they would lead him, but was quite willing to submit for a final decision of the truth to faith and authority.

The contrast is significant, and it seems to disclose a genuine alternative, given the different premises of both thinkers, and of their respective philosophical traditions. I hope I have been able to show that each of them succeeded in developing a suggestive view of the world and of life, and, as it were, in making a good case for his own position. I shall not attempt to arbitrate between these two world views, which have been recurrent in one form or another throughout the history of Western thought, and each of which seems to reflect one of the basic experiences or options of which human nature and thought are capable. Let it be enough to say that both thinkers found very dignified formulations for their respective views, and met with the approval of many contemporaries and successors. Renaissance Aristotelianism culminates as much in Pomponazzi as Renaissance Platonism had found its fullest expression in Ficino.

Pomponazzi's influence is not so easily traced as that of Ficino or Pico, but there is ample evidence to show that it was considerable. The school of Italian Aristotelianism to which he belonged flourished for another hundred years or more after his death, and within this tradition his name remained famous, and his views on such questions as the immortality of the soul and the unity of the intellect continued to be cited and discussed, if not adopted. The posthumous publication of several of his writings later in the century also gives testimony to his continued fame. The number of manuscripts in which his lectures and questions were copied is quite large, as compared with most other professors of philosophy of the time, an indication of his popularity among his students; moreover, the considerable number of manuscripts containing the *De incantationibus* and the *De fato* proves that these works circulated widely, although, or perhaps because, they were not published during the author's lifetime. A few anecdotes associated with his name, as we find them in the biographies, short stories, and dialogues of the period, suggest that as a character he made some impression even on the larger public outside university circles. Obviously he was read by students and writers who did not belong to the Aristotelian tradition, and we may cite as an example the unfortunate Giulio Cesare Vanini, who seems to have used him as one of his favorite sources.[13]

During the seventeenth century, the Aristotelian school that had dominated the teaching of philosophy for such a long time finally lost its hold, especially in the field of natural philosophy, which was gradually replaced by the new mathematical physics of Galileo and his successors. For early modern physics did not develop out of nothing in the seventeenth century, as some historians seem to believe; it replaced Aristotelian physics, as a result of one of the most momentous revolutions that ever affected the history of thought, the academic curriculum, and the classification of the sciences. Aristotelianism resisted much longer in the fields of logic, biology, and metaphysics, and it attained its greatest triumphs in the field of poetics during the same seventeenth century in which its physics suffered final defeat. Yet since physics was the center and stronghold of medieval and Renaissance Aristotelianism, especially in Italy, most of Pomponazzi's specific teachings lost their immediate validity when the Aristotelian system within which he had developed his ideas came to be abandoned. Nevertheless, we may say that his view of the relation between natural reason and faith was capable of being reformulated in terms of the new physics, and that in certain instances this did in fact happen.

Even greater importance may be attributed to another development. The seventeenth century, and even more the eighteenth, witnessed the rise and diffusion of free thought and overt atheism, especially in France, and some of the free thinkers who set out to discard faith and established religion came to consider the Aristotelian rationalists such as Pomponazzi as their forerunners and allies. Pomponazzi's treatise on the immortality of the soul was praised by the free thinkers, and condemned by Catholic apologists, while moderate thinkers like Bayle tried to preserve a proper perspective.[14] Pomponazzi's treatise was even reprinted in a clandestine edition with a false early date. We are reminded of the notorious book on the three impostors that was cited by many medieval and Renaissance authors, and attributed to many writers including Pomponazzi, but never existed until it was finally written in the eighteenth century and published with a false sixteenth-century imprint.

This use to which the French Enlightenment put Pomponazzi and the other Italian Aristotelians has had a strong influence on modern historians of the school, beginning with Renan, whose book on Averroism celebrated its centenary about ten years ago. Again we must make a distinction. It is one thing to say that Pomponazzi and the Aristotelians held the same views as later free thinkers, and another to state that they represent an earlier phase in a development that in one of its later phases was to produce the views held by the free thinkers. In the latter sense, Pomponazzi was a forerunner of the free thinkers; in the former sense, I am convinced, he was not. Hence we should not praise or blame him, depending on our own preferences and values, for being a free thinker, since we lack the factual basis for either judgment. Yet in a different sense we may praise or blame him, and I am inclined to praise him. He belongs to the long line of thinkers who have attempted to draw a clear line of distinction between reason and faith, philosophy and theology, and to establish the autonomy of reason and philosophy within their own domain, unassailable by the demands of any faith, or of any claim not based on reason. All those of us who have a stake in reason, that is, not merely in science, but in philosophy and any kind of knowledge, should be grateful for this attitude, and embrace it ourselves. If we have a faith that is not based on reason, we shall at least keep it apart, and not allow it to interfere with the dictates of reason. If we have no such faith, we can at least tolerate, outside the precincts of reason, the faith cherished by others, knowing that no inroads can be made upon the territory within which we feel at home. There are many faiths, and we may not share that of others, as others may not share ours, or we may not even share any faith whatsoever. But all men without exception may share in reason and its conquests, and it should be our common concern to extend its domain as far as we can, and not to accept any attempt to reduce it. Our life and our person are not made of reason alone, and the more we are aware of this fact, the better it is. But reason is the only tool we have for bringing a ray of light and order into the great, dark chaos from which we were born, into which we shall return, and by which we are surrounded on all sides.

6

Telesio

The thinkers whom we shall discuss in the three remaining chapters were all active during the second half of the sixteenth century, and what separates them from those we have considered so far is not merely the passing of a few decades, but the emergence of a completely different intellectual atmosphere. The tradition of medieval thought, which was still felt very strongly in the fifteenth century and even at the beginning of the sixteenth, began to recede into the more distant background, and it was now the broad thought and learning of the early Renaissance itself which constituted the tradition by which the new generations of thinkers were shaped, and against which their immediate reactions were directed.

Moreover, the sixteenth century witnessed an event, or rather a series of events, which effected one of the most profound changes and reorientations that have ever occurred in the history of European thought, and which may be considered the most important event of the whole period: the Reformation. Within a few decades, its repercussions were felt in all countries and regions of Europe, and affected all areas of European life and culture; its consequences have lasted up to this very day. No wonder that many historians have tended to start with the Reformation an entirely new period of European history, and to regard the beginning of the Reformation, or some slightly later event such as the sack of Rome, as the end of that Renaissance, which found its characteristic expression in the fifteenth century and the early years of the sixteenth, but could not have developed in the climate of the Reformation, and hence had to make room, after the advent of the Reformation, for different attitudes and modes of thought.

Actually, the record of the hundred years or so following the Reformation looks grim enough for the cultural historian who is not merely satisfied with extolling the merits and victories of his favorite among the contesting religious parties, and we are sadly reminded of the ravages brought about by the national and ideological conflicts of our own time. The annals of Europe are full of foreign and civil wars caused by the religious dissensions of the sixteenth century. Religious opponents were persecuted everywhere without hesitation or mercy. They were imprisoned, tortured, and killed, or forced to recant under humiliating circumstances. Those who did not wish to submit, and managed to save their lives, had to flee from their homes into exile, and some of them were forced to move from one foreign country to another. Those who stayed at home and wished to remain undisturbed had to conform, at least outwardly, to whatever religious opinion the authorities of their country approved, and had to avoid in their conduct, and especially in their writings, anything that might give offense or seem to smack of heresy. The record of Spain was especially somber. There was tolerance in Holland, and for a limited time in Poland, yet the cases of More and Servetus show that the Protestants were as capable of persecution as the Catholics, when they happened to be in power. Whatever our religious preferences may be, and however much we may respect and even admire Luther or Calvin or Ignatius of Loyola, as scholars and philosophers we cannot help sympathizing with Erasmus, who was trying to keep himself, and the cause of learning, out of the violent turmoil of religious controversy.

We may have reason to feel sympathy, not only with the victims, but also with the persecutors (who often acted in good faith, in a sincere though wrong belief that they were doing their duty), and we may sometimes approve the views of the latter, and reject those of the former. Yet we cannot help being repelled by the spectacle of people being cruelly punished or executed for holding religious beliefs different from those of their rulers. A person must be punished for public crimes, for breaking the ordinary laws of his country and society. A religious community has the right to exclude from its ranks those who cease to share its basic beliefs. An established government, whatever its origin or nature, cannot help defending its institutions against those trying to overthrow it, although its moral right to do so will in the end be judged on the basis of whatever moral substance this government and its institutions possess, that is, on the basis of their accordance with a higher and more universal principle of morality. But as scholars and thinkers we must maintain (and unfortunately it is timely to say this again) that it is wrong to punish a person for his religious or philosophical or even political opinions alone.

In the later sixteenth century, Italy was not directly involved in religious wars, but she had her sad share in religious persecution, and in the censorship and suppression of religious opinion. The Spanish Inquisition and the Congregation of the Index were firmly established, and the decrees of the Council of Trent were fully enforced and applied. Protestant sympathizers were imprisoned and executed, including more than one notable scholar. Others were forced into exile, and there is a sizable list of distinguished scholars who went to foreign countries on account of their religious opinions, especially to Switzerland, Germany, England, and Poland. Many others were forced to recant, or to submit their writings to censorship, and to make changes in their works before they were published; some (we do not know how many) anticipated such censorship, or kept entirely silent. This situation affected not only religious and theological opinions in the narrow sense of the words, but also those philosophical and scientific views that seemed to have a bearing on theology. Thus we find many thinkers more or less seriously involved with the Inquisition, although they cannot be said to have been sympathetic to Protestantism, or interested in the problems that stood at the center of the religious controversies. This is true of Patrizi as well as of Campanella, Cremonini, and Galileo, not to mention the tragic case of Bruno, as we shall see in the last chapter.

Yet after all this has been said, we must be careful to avoid certain exaggerated conclusions that have been drawn by many historians. It simply is not true that the position of an Erasmus became completely hopeless, say, after 1525, or that independent thought and scholarship became impossible after the Reformation. Actually, the tradition of humanist scholarship continued unimpaired, and perhaps there was more independent philosophical speculation after the Reformation than there had been during the earlier Renaissance.

The explanation for these facts is very simple. Human thought and knowledge have many compartments and extend into many dimensions. The totalitarian claim of theological orthodoxy, if it was ever made, could no more be enforced than that of political orthodoxy today. There was and is a large territory of philosophical thought, science, and scholarship that is theologically and politically neutral, and that has always been cultivated by persons of diverse religious and political allegiances. There is such a thing as the autonomy of culture, and it has always been the task and duty of scholars to defend this territory against the deeper inroads of religious and political influences, whereas the outer fringes of the territory are always open to these influences. I hope I have made it clear that I am far from underestimating the impact of the Reformation on the intellectual life of the later sixteenth century, but also that I consider it possible to study the history of scholarship, science, and philosophy during that period apart from its religious and political developments.

The thinkers with whom we shall deal in these remaining chapters are usually referred to, along with a number of other thinkers in Italy and elsewhere, as the Renaissance philosophers of nature; they are considered a group by themselves, different from the humanists, Platonists, and Aristotelians discussed so far. The label suggests that the central interest of these men was in natural philosophy and cosmology, as that of the early humanist thinkers had been in ethics. Yet what distinguished the philosophers of nature from the Platonists and Aristotelians of their time, or of the preceding generations, was not so much the broad subject matter of their thought as their endeavor and claim to explore the principles of nature in an original and independent way, rather than within the framework of an established tradition and authority. They tried to formulate novel theories, and were proud to free themselves from the ancient philosophical authorities, especially from Aristotle, who had dominated philosophical speculation, and in particular natural philosophy, for the past several centuries. This claim appears in their polemics and in their prefaces, and at times in the very titles of their works.

In the face of a well-established tradition, this attitude shows considerable courage and even boldness. What was involved we may see in the case of Cardano, who thought it was one of his main achievements that he had reduced the traditional scheme of the four elements to three by denying to the element of fire its customary status.[1] The quest for originality reflects a conviction which began to develop at this time, and which was to reach much larger dimensions in the seventeenth century, namely, that it was possible for the moderns to make new discoveries and to attain knowledge that had not been accessible to the ancients.[2] The sixteenth century actually witnessed in mathematics and astronomy, anatomy and botany, the first tangible advances beyond the ancients, and the invention of printing as well as the discovery of America began to be used as arguments for the superiority of the moderns.

As might be expected, the new philosophers of nature were not so original or so independent of ancient authorities as they claimed to be, just as the professed Platonists or Aristotelians, for that matter, were not such faithful followers of their ancient authorities as they believed themselves to be. In the philosophers of nature, we shall encounter more than once reflections of Aristotelian, Platonist, and other ancient, medieval, or humanist ideas that are not merely undigested residuals of an obsolete tradition, but quite essential ingredients of the new thought. Yet the attitude remains significant, and it is for their independent outlook as much as for their particular theories that the philosophers of nature have often been hailed as forerunners of modern philosophy and science.

What separates them from the early modern scientists, and from the philosophers of the seventeenth century who took the new science as their premise, is their failure to find a firm and valid method of natural inquiry, and especially to understand the fundamental importance of mathematics for such a method. It was for this reason, rather than on account of the dead weight of obsolete traditions, that their brilliant and impressive constructions remained more or less isolated, and failed to gain a wide following or to affect the university teaching of natural philosophy, which remained firmly under the control of the Aristotelians. The Aristotelian tradition of natural philosophy was not overthrown by the outside attacks of the humanists or Platonists, nor by the suggestive theories of the natural philosophers. It yielded only in and after the seventeenth century, when the new science of Galileo and his successors was able to deal with its subject matter on the basis of a firmly established and superior method.

Bernardino Telesio was not the earliest of the independent natural philosophers of the sixteenth century. He was preceded in Italy by the humanist Girolamo Fracastoro and the polyhistor Girolamo Cardano, and in Germany by the physician and occultist Theophrastus Paracelsus, to mention but a few of the more famous names. I have chosen to treat Telesio in preference to these others because his thought is distinguished by a certain measure of clarity and coherence, and because some of his ideas anticipate important aspects of later philosophy.

Telesio was born in Cosenza in 1509, and in a sense he opens the long line of philosophers through which the South of Italy has asserted its Greek heritage, a line that links him with Bruno and Campanella, with Vico in the eighteenth century, and with Croce and Gentile in our own time. Telesio was educated in Milan and Rome by his uncle, the humanist Antonio Telesio, and studied philosophy and mathematics at the university of Padua, where he obtained his doctorate in 1535. He seems to have spent the next few years in a monastery in Calabria, occupied with his studies and thoughts, which began to move away from the Aristotelian tradition of his upbringing. He married in 1553 and had four children; his wife died in 1561. After many hesitations, he published the first edition of his main work, *De rerum natura iuxta propria principia*, in Naples in 1565. This edition is divided into two books, which correspond to the first four books of the final version. In 1570, he published a slightly revised second edition, adding several shorter treatises on specific questions of natural philosophy. After he had received a certain amount of recognition from several philosophers in northern and central Italy, he finally published a third and much enlarged edition of the work in 1586. This edition is divided into nine books, and it forms the basis of the modern critical edition. Shortly afterwards, Telesio was deeply shaken by the tragic death of one of his sons, and he died in Cosenza in 1588. A number of his shorter works were published posthumously in 1590.

Telesio never taught at a university, although he received at least one offer from Rome. However, in his home town Cosenza, in which he spent a large part of his later years except for several long visits to Naples, he founded after the custom of the period an Academy, the Accademia Cosentina, dedicated to the study of natural philosophy according to his principles and methods. He seems to have done a certain amount of teaching here; in any case, he had several pupils, and the Academy continued its activities for a certain number of years after his death.

In discussing Telesio's thought, it will be best to give a short summary of his main work, *De rerum natura,* drawing upon the definitive third edition, which is by far the most complete. In his Preface, Telesio rejects Aristotle's doctrine as being in conflict with the senses, with itself, and with Scripture, and claims that his own doctrine is free from these defects.[3] In the Introduction to the first book, he insists again that unlike his predecessors, who merely followed their own inventions, he has followed nothing but sense perception and nature, but adds that he is willing to subordinate even the testimony of the senses to the authority of Scripture and the Catholic Church.[4]

He then proceeds to expound the principles of his natural philosophy, and posits heat and cold as the two active principles of all things, with matter as a third, passive, principle. Heaven, and especially the sun, represents the principle of heat, and the earth the principle of cold, and out of their cooperation all other things are generated (I, 1–5).

Having developed and applied these principles in some detail, Telesio concludes the first book of his work with an interesting treatment of space and time (I, 25–29). Using the water clock and other observable phenomena as examples, Telesio argues against Aristotle that an empty space is possible, and defines space as something that is capable of containing bodies, and distinct from the bodies which it contains (I, 25). This space is without motion, identical throughout, can exist without bodies, and is that in which all beings are located. In defending this view, Telesio appeals to the testimony of the senses against the reasons of Aristotle. Similarly, he argues against Aristotle that time is not dependent on motion, and that all motion presupposes time and occurs within time (I, 29).

Having set forth his own position, Telesio examines and refutes the views of the earlier philosophers, in particular Aristotle and his followers, whom he considers superior to all others in this branch of philosophy. The critique of Aristotelianism occupies the next three books, and this is the section with which the work was concluded in its first two editions.

Evidently the doctrine summarized so far constitutes the earliest core of Telesio's philosophy, and the theories set forth in the later books were written up, if not conceived, at a later stage of his development. Broadly speaking, we may say that the first four books deal with cosmology, and the last five books with biological, and especially psychological, questions. The entire discussion hinges on a fundamental distinction introduced by Telesio in the fifth book and maintained throughout the remainder of the work (V, 2).

According to this distinction, there are two different souls in man. Telesio calls the first of them the spirit produced from the seed, and the second the soul infused by God. The first, the spirit, as we shall call it for short, is also found in animals and even in plants. It is a kind of tenuous, subtle body, and must be regarded not merely as the form of the body, as Aristotle believed, but rather as a thing existing by itself. It is located primarily in the brain, but from there it is diffused through the entire body. An animal thus consists of spirit and body as of two distinct and diverse things, and the spirit is enclosed in the body as in a cover or organ. Now the first function of the spirit, we are told in Book VII, is sensation, and hence sensation is attributed to all things on account of the spirit. The spirit has sensation because it is acted upon and changed by external things, and is aware of these changes and passions that affect it. Thus the spirit perceives external things insofar as it senses its own changes and passions, which are in turn caused by those external things (VII, 2).

The effect of external things upon the spirit consists in expansion or in contraction, and these impulses may be conducive to the preservation or the corruption of the spirit. Hence sensation is immediately accompanied by pleasure or pain, since pleasure is nothing but the

99

sense of preservation, and pain nothing but the sense of corruption (VII, 3).

All sensation is ultimately derived from the sense of touch (VII, 8). With this principle in mind, Telesio discusses in Book VIII the various forms of knowledge. The spirit perceives all things, he repeats, because it is acted upon and moved by all things, and thus it also perceives their similarity and dissimilarity. By perceiving objects as being identical or different, the spirit arrives at universal concepts (VIII, 1). For the spirit possesses, besides sensation, the faculty of memory or retention (VIII, 2). Now all knowledge consists in passing from that which is completely known to that which is known only in part. When reason posits anything, it does so on the basis of a similarity with things perceived, and it rejects whatever is in contrast with its perceptions. Thus the basis of all intellectual knowledge is a similarity perceived by the senses.[5] Intellectual knowledge is hence derived from sense perception, and is less perfect than the latter (VIII, 3). Even geometry is based on sense perception (VIII, 4), and mathematical conclusions are inferior to those of natural philosophy (VIII, 5). Since our thought is subject to fatigue, error, and forgetfulness, this proves that it is performed with the cooperation of the spirit, which is subject to such defects, even though the higher soul may also be involved. Pure thought, without the cooperation of the spirit, will be possible only in a future life (VIII, 6). All our knowledge, insofar as it is related to natural objects and derived from them, is thus based on perception and on the similarity of its objects (VIII, 7). This knowledge and this reason, since they are related to perception, are also shared by the animals (VIII, 14).

On the other hand, man possesses a higher soul, which is created by God and infused into his body, in particular into his spirit, and this soul possesses a different faculty of thinking that is peculiar to it. Thus man has two souls, one divine and immortal, the other corporeal and mortal. Consequently, man has a twofold desire and a twofold intellect. One intellect perceives things divine, belongs to the infused soul, and is peculiar to man. The other intellect perceives sense objects, belongs to the spirit, and is possessed also by the animals. We might better reserve the name "intellect" for the former, and call the latter the faculty of knowing and remembering. On account of his twofold desire, man possesses free will, which is not shared by the animals (VIII, 15). The intellect of the infused soul is incorporeal and has no corporeal instrument; it is merely passive and potential in relation to its objects. It receives the forms of its objects, and it is related to intelligible things in the same way that perception is related to sense objects (VIII, 19).

After this digression on the infused soul, which is mainly contained in Book VIII, Telesio returns to the spirit, and tries to build upon it a detailed theory of the passions, and of the virtues and vices. Differences in intelligence and moral character among human beings are attributed to the differences in their spirits with respect to warmth, subtlety, and purity (VIII, 35–36). The spirit is ruled by the principle of self-preservation (IX, 3), and pleasure is nothing but the sense of this preservation, as we have already seen. Our passions and emotions reflect the changes to which our spirit is exposed, and the self-preservation of the spirit constitutes the measure of these emotions. Moderate emotions constitute virtue, since they correspond to favorable impulses received by the spirit that are conducive to its preservation, whereas immoderate emotions constitute vice, since they correspond to harmful impulses conducive to the corruption of the spirit (IX, 4). Telesio concludes his work with a detailed discussion of particular virtues and vices on the basis of these principles.

I have intentionally refrained from interrupting this summary of Telesio's system with my own comments in order to convey its apparent force and coherence. However, if we examine these ideas more closely, a number of problems become evident. So far as Telesio's relation to Aristotle is concerned, we must admit that he shows considerable independence, both in his own theories and in his detailed criticism of Aristotle's views, and this independence is the more valuable since it is based not on ignorance, but on a thorough knowledge of the Aristotelian writings, and is accompanied by a genuine respect for the relative merits of Aristotelianism.[6] The only other sources that Telesio quotes at any length seem to be the medical authorities, Hippocrates and Galen, and this suggests that he probably studied medicine at Padua, as well as philosophy and mathematics, though he did not attain a degree in this subject. From these and later medical authorities he evidently drew his detailed notions of the human body, its parts and functions, as they appear in the physiological sections of his work.

His concept of the spirit as a subtle body is likewise indebted to the medical tradition, and probably also to the Stoic concept of *pneuma*, which could have been known to him from a variety of ancient sources. The attempt to treat pleasure and pain as primary feelings closely linked with sensation is reminiscent of Epicurus; yet Telesio does not seem to link virtue directly with pleasure, but relates them both to the principle of self-preservation, which has its closest counterpart again in the Stoics. His extreme sensationalism, which treats perception as the only basis of knowledge, may also be compared with Stoic and Epicurean ideas, whereas the more detailed attempt to derive universals from the perceived similarities between sense objects reflects the views of his older contemporary Fracastoro. The acceptance of heat, cold, and matter as principles of the physical world has no exact counterpart in pre-Socratic thought, as one might think at first glance. It is, rather, a more specific version of the triad of matter, form, and privation that appears in Aristotle's *Physics* (I, 7), whereas the distinction between active and passive principles again sounds Stoic.

Finally, the distinction between the two souls and their corresponding faculties of knowing and desiring is distinctly Neoplatonic, and may also be indebted to Ficino, although the manner in which Telesio distributes our faculties between the two souls does not precisely correspond to the views of these predecessors. When he calls the higher soul infused or created, he obviously borrows from theology, but otherwise there are few traces of specific theological doctrines in his philosophy, except for the submission to the Church expressed in his Introduction.

These apparent borrowings from various sources certainly should not be overlooked, but one's final impression is that in transforming and combining these ideas, and in formulating some important new ones, Telesio was remarkably original. In his cosmology, the role assigned to heat, cold, and matter is chiefly of historical interest, since it is one of the first serious attempts to replace Aristotle's natural philosophy. We may give him credit, too, for apparently doing away with the sharp distinction between celestial and terrestrial phenomena, which was one of the chief weaknesses of the Aristotelian system. Of greater significance are his theories of the void, and of space and time. His assertion of an empty space was in a sense a return to the position of the ancient atomists, which Aristotle had tried to refute; this position must have been known to Telesio, from Lucretius and also from Aristotle himself, but the evidence on which he based himself was partly new and, so to speak, experimental.

Still more important is his theory of space and time. Whereas Aristotle had defined time as the number or measure of motion, thus making it dependent on motion, Telesio regards time as independent of, and prior to, motion, like an empty receptacle. He thus moves a long step away from Aristotle in the direction of Newton's absolute time.

In the case of space, the change in conception is even more interesting. The Greek term "topos," which we often translate as space, has the primary meaning of place, and Aristotle's theory that the "topos" of the contained body is the limit or border of its containing body makes much better sense when we translate "topos" as place rather than space. Telesio seems to be aware of this ambiguity, for he uses not only the term "locus," which had been the standard Latin translation of Aristotle's "topos," but also "spatium," which is much more appropriate for his own notion of an empty space in which all bodies are contained. Thus he again moves away from Aristotle in the direction of Newton's absolute space; but, more than this, I am tempted to believe that it was Telesio himself who gave terminological precision to the word "spatium" (space) and substituted it for "locus," a usage for which I do not know any earlier clear instances (although I may just be ignorant of them).[7] This would tend to confirm once more the principle that seems to be often valid in the history of ideas and of terms, namely that a specific term is usually coined within the context of a system in which the idea expressed by that term is for the first time conceived, and in which the need for such a term arises for the first time and with a kind of necessity. It also illustrates the way in which the specific meanings of ordinary English terms are not always rooted in present usage, as it is fixed in dictionaries of the twentieth century, but frequently in the quite extraordinary thought and language of past philosophers who expressed themselves in extraordinary Greek or Latin terms, which in the course of the centuries filtered down and were transformed into the ordinary terms of English, French, or German, or of any other modern language spoken by a people that had the privilege of inheriting some of its thoughts and words from the Greek philosophers of antiquity, and from the Latin philosophers of medieval and early modern times.

We may also give Telesio credit for treating space and time as a pair of concepts that belong together, that must be discussed in an analogous fashion, and that are somehow distinct in status from all other groups of ideas. Aristotle, to be sure, treats both place and time in his *Physics*, but he does not treat the two concepts along completely parallel lines. In the fourth book of the *Physics*, the discussion of place and that of time are separated by a discussion of the void, which is not treated merely as a part of the section on place.[8] In giving a special status to space and time, Telesio again anticipates Newton, and in this instance also Leibniz and Kant.

Finally, a significant contribution is Telesio's radical theory of knowledge, which reduces everything to sense perception. His attempt to derive even reason and its universal concepts from sensation had its precedents, as we have seen, but it is far more consistently developed, and it may very well be considered as a source and precedent for Francis Bacon and the British Empiricists. Bacon knew Telesio's work, and he criticized it rather sharply, both for its specific ideas and for its supposed failure to apply its professed criterion of sense perception. Yet when Bacon called Telesio "the first of the moderns," he must have thought of his emphasis on sense perception, and of his independence from Aristotle, and must have considered him in these respects to be his own predecessor.[9]

Telesio's notion that sensation originally belongs to the spirit, a material entity, does not seem satisfactory, since it begs the question how sensation, or consciousness, can be derived from a material being. It was in a sense a return to the hylozoism of the pre-Socratics, or to the materialism of the Stoics, whose *pneuma* Telesio's spirit resembles in so many ways. Presumably he found the notion helpful because it simplified his scheme of natural principles, and permitted him to link much of his epistemology, psychology, and ethics with his physical theories. This notion was taken up and further developed by a famous disciple of his, Campanella, who at least in his early period maintained that all matter is immediately endowed with sensation.[10]

Telesio's doctrine of the two souls has puzzled many of his interpreters, for his introduction of the higher soul seems to break the continuity and coherence of his otherwise naturalistic system, and to add to it conceptions of Platonist and theological origin that appear to be hardly compatible with the rest of his thought. As usual, some historians have argued that Telesio was not sincere in making this addition, but merely tried to appease possible theological critics and opponents. The fear of the Inquisition was no doubt a more serious factor in Telesio's time than it had been a century before, or even for Pomponazzi, yet I can see no real evidence for the view that the doctrine of the higher soul was not seriously stated and endorsed by Telesio. Even if we assume that he felt he had to make a concession, we may wonder why he made so few others. For an unfriendly critic, the work as it stands contains plenty of objectionable statements whose significance is by no means diminished by this supposed concession. I see no difficulty in assuming that Telesio was a good Catholic, and that he found it necessary to posit a higher soul, besides the spirit, in order to establish that the human soul was immortal and related to God. We must also note that he distributed our functions between the two souls in a very specific manner which differed from the views of all his predecessors, so far as I can see. For he assigns to the lower soul not only our biological functions, sense perception, and memory, but also our reasoning and cognitive faculty insofar as it is concerned with natural objects. The knowledge of intelligible or divine objects is not related to sensation, and hence belongs not to the spirit, but to the higher soul. When Telesio says that a pure knowledge of divine objects will be possible only in the afterlife, and that in the present life the higher soul, if it thinks in us, does so only with the cooperation of the spirit, I should not infer that he actually denies the possibility of an impure knowledge of the divine during the present life. Yet even if we regret the addition of the doctrine of the higher soul, we must still be surprised at the length to which he was able to go in extending the limits of his naturalistic principles.

To assess Telesio's influence and historical significance, we must repeat and supplement some of the remarks we have made already. Through his writings and his Academy, Telesio aroused the attention, and gained the respect, of many contemporaries, and we find him cited and criticized by such important thinkers as Patrizi[11] and Bacon. He also had a small number of later pupils and followers, notably the young Campanella (1568–1639), who spent the last years of his life in France and acquired a very wide reputation, both through the vicissitudes of his life and through his extensive literary production. Finally, in some of his characteristic theories, Telesio appears as a direct or indirect forerunner of Newton and Locke. To be called a forerunner of some great modern thinker is no longer the unadulterated praise it used to be, and there may even be some irony to it. As long as historians were convinced that modern thought and civilization followed a continuous curve of steady progress, to be called the forerunner of some later thinker was the greatest honor that could be bestowed upon a philosopher of the past. He was taken out of the regrettable backwardness of his own time and elevated to the company of a more advanced and enlightened century. Our cynical age, however, has lost this happy faith in continuous and, as it were, inevitable progress. The only inevitable progress seems to be technological, and even that appears at times to be a mixed blessing. All other progress must be gained by hard effort, and sometimes by fighting; if it is attained, it is dearly paid for, and even then it may easily be lost again.

This doubt about continuous progress applies particularly to the history of philosophy. For instance, I happen not to consider Locke the ultimate authority in philosophy or epistemology, although I do respect his work and his person, and therefore I should not consider it such high praise for Telesio to be called his precursor. To have been a precursor of Kant or Hegel would get a much higher score with me, and some of my colleagues may have still different tastes and preferences. Even natural science has its changes and revolutions, and what seemed to be the last word a little while ago, suddenly appears antiquated, and makes room for a quite different conception. As long as Newton's notions of space and time were generally accepted, it certainly appeared high praise for Telesio to be described as his forerunner; now that Newton's conceptions have been replaced by those of Einstein and others, the description would seem to have lost much of its merit. Historians ought to be more careful in holding up a thinker of the past as a forerunner of the latest fashion in philosophy or in science; this will not benefit him tomorrow, when these systems have themselves become a matter of the past, and quite different ones are the order of the day.

However, in the case of Telesio and Newton, I am of a somewhat different opinion. It is true that Newton has been superseded by Einstein, but this does not mean that Newton has suddenly become all wrong, or that Aristotle has suddenly become a forerunner of Einstein, or scored, as it were, a belated victory over Newton. Natural science is making steady progress, for it accumulates its evidence, and each theory marks a progress over its predecessor insofar as it accounts in a more satisfactory way for all the evidence that is available at the time it is formulated. The external similarity between different theories does not really matter. What matters is the amount of empirical and rational evidence on which the respective theory is based. Aristotle's physics was respectable for its time and sufficient for many subsequent centuries. When it failed to satisfy the evidence available in the seventeenth century, it was superseded, for good, by the physics of Galileo and Newton. In the same way, Newton's physics has been superseded by that of the twentieth century because it failed to account for the additional evidence which had become available. This does not give any merit or comfort to Aristotle, whose knowledge of physics was much less than Newton's, and whose system has by no means been revived, although a few of its tenets may have some remote or superficial resemblances with present-day physics.

Thus after all, it may be a praise for Telesio to be called a predecessor of Newton, especially since he did discover some of the weaknesses of the Aristotelian physics, and since he may have exerted at least an indirect influence on Newton. Yet I think it is still higher praise when we say of Telesio that he was a respectable thinker in his own right, who deserves our admiration for the honesty and originality of his effort, and who managed to give one of the typical and recurrent philosophical positions a novel, and in a sense classical, formulation.

7

Patrizi

Francesco Patrizi was twenty years younger than Telesio, but he died
not very long after him, before the end of the sixteenth century, and
may therefore be regarded as his contemporary. The two thinkers
were apparently engaged in a friendly correspondence, for we have
a letter from Patrizi to Telesio in which he formulates an acute criticism of the latter's philosophical principles.[1] We may also say of Patrizi, as of Telesio, that he attempted to develop a systematic explanation of the physical universe, and to do so in a new and original way,
independent of, and contrary to, the Aristotelian tradition. It is significant that his chief work is entitled "A New Philosophy of the
Universe" (*Nova de universis philosophia,* 1591). So there are good
reasons for grouping Patrizi, along with Telesio and a number of
other Italian and European thinkers of the sixteenth century, among
the Renaissance philosophers of nature, who were unattached to the
classical traditions of Western thought and prepared the way for the
new science and the new philosophy of the seventeenth century and
modern times.

However, when we pass from the writings and ideas of Telesio to
those of Patrizi, we find ourselves in a completely different world. It
is not merely that their opinions on specific problems differ widely,
but that their premises, their problems and the emphasis they place
on different areas of thought and knowledge are miles apart. The
philosophers of nature, unlike the humanists and Aristotelians, and

even unlike the Platonists, did not form a unified group or school in which a variety of ideas or interests would be possible, but which would always be held together by a common institutional or doctrinal tradition. The lack of such a tradition, and the quest for novel and original approaches and solutions, led to a much greater variety and discontinuity in ideas and systems among the philosophers of nature than we have encountered among the representatives of the other schools, in spite of a broad affinity that we may discover in their themes and aspirations, and perhaps in the style of their thinking.

From another point of view, this diversity among the philosophers of nature is connected with the place philosophy occupies within the intellectual globe. Philosophy is no doubt comprehensive and universal in its scope and aspirations, but its attachment to other branches of thought and knowledge, and the relative importance it attributes to them, varies greatly among different schools and at different periods. It makes a great deal of difference whether philosophers are concerned primarily with religion and theology, or with the sciences, or with art and literature, or with historical knowledge, and even whether their concern with the sciences is centered upon mathematics or physics or biology. The preoccupation with these non-philosophical areas of thought will determine in the case of each philosopher, not only his general orientation, but the relative importance he gives in his system to the various philosophical disciplines.

We have seen that the humanists were oriented toward literature and classical studies, and cultivated among the philosophical disciplines primarily, if not exclusively, the field of ethics. The Aristotelians were mainly concerned with physics, biology, and medicine, and hence they concentrated on the field of natural philosophy, which was still considered a part of philosophy rather than a special science. Our philosophers of nature, in spite of their name, were not limited in their interests to the natural philosophy of the Aristotelians, or to what was to become the physics of the moderns, although they deal

III

in part with analogous problems and stand historically halfway between these two traditions. They differ among each other even in this general intellectual orientation. Telesio was primarily a student of the physical and biological sciences, to which his ideas on ethics and epistemology seem to be subordinated, and in this broad sense he belongs to the Aristotelian tradition in which he was brought up, and from which he inherited his problems and themes, although he was to abandon and to criticize most of the specific solutions and theories it offered. Patrizi, by contrast, does not share this primary interest in physics, biology, and medicine, or the corresponding attachment, negative though it was, to the Aristotelian tradition. His outside interests are on the one hand literary and classical, and on the other mathematical. These different interests, and their rather unusual combination, go a long way to explain his different historical attachments, which are humanist and Platonist rather than Aristotelian, and the different style and emphasis of his system, even at those points where he does try to answer the problems of natural philosophy. Fracastoro was a humanist and a physician, Cardano a physician and a mathematician, Paracelsus a physician and an alchemist, Bruno a literary writer, a natural philosopher, and a metaphysician (but hardly a mathematician), and Campanella, among many other things, a theologian and a political thinker.

In other words, the Renaissance philosophers of nature differ among each other, not only in their opinions but also in the structure and orientation of their thought, much more widely than is ordinarily the case within a single school or group of philosophers. Finally, compared with the humanists and Aristotelians, and even with the Platonists of the Renaissance period, they represent a rather small group of more or less isolated figures. None of them, not even Telesio, had a large following. The prominent place they occupy in Renaissance thought does not depend on their number, or the number of their pupils, but on the intrinsic quality of their contribution, the influence they had on later thought, and their historical place as harbingers, if not predecessors in the strict sense, of early modern science and philosophy.

Francesco Patrizi was born in 1529 at Cherso in Istria, near Trieste. He studied at Ingolstadt, and from 1547 to 1554 at Padua, apparently philosophy and the humanities. For the years after 1550, the details of his life are not known too well. He served several Venetian noblemen as a secretary and administrator, and must have spent many years in Venice, where a number of his writings were published between 1553 and 1572. His affairs took him repeatedly to Cyprus, and perhaps to other parts of the Greek-speaking world, and it is in this period that he must have acquired the mastery of the Greek language that distinguished him during his later years. Afterwards, probably in the 1570's, he spent some time in Spain, where he sold many of his Greek manuscripts to King Philip II. After his return from Spain, he stayed for some time in Modena and Ferrara. In 1578, Duke Alfonso II appointed him professor of Platonic philosophy at the University of Ferrara, a position especially created for him upon his request. He held this chair for many years, lecturing on Plato's *Republic* and on Platonic philosophy in general. In 1592, he was called by Pope Clement VIII to the University of Rome, again as professor of Platonic philosophy, and there he lectured mainly on the *Timaeus*. During the following years, he planned to republish his major work, and defended his views before the Congregation of the Index, which insisted on a number of changes and finally condemned the work. He died in 1597, before he had attained his goal of having a new version approved.

Patrizi's numerous published writings show a great variety of interests. He wrote a poem in Italian, annotated the poems of Luca Contile, and edited Girolamo Ruscelli's book on devices (*imprese*). An anonymous Italian version of a collection of fables, originally composed in India but translated from the Greek, must probably be attributed to him.[2] He gave a lecture on a sonnet of Petrarch, and became involved in the literary controversies of his time, publishing a pamphlet in favor of Ariosto,[3] and replying to the criticism directed against him by Torquato Tasso and Jacopo Mazzoni. These writings, as well as his Italian dialogue on honor, correspond to the intellectual interests of the literary Academies of the period, as does the recently published, fragmentary dialogue on the philosophy of love, which is much less "Platonic" than one might have expected.[4] He also composed in Italian two antiquarian works dealing with the military art of the Romans.

Patrizi's treatises on poetics, rhetoric, and the art of history obviously belong together, for the three subjects were linked in the theoretical literature of the sixteenth century, and already before then in the program of the *studia humanitatis,* although the humanists did not produce many separate treatises on these subjects, with the exception of rhetoric. Patrizi's "Art of History" (*Della historia,* 1560) is interesting as a contribution to a genre that was still fairly new at the time, and that may be considered as the first beginning of later literature on the methodology and philosophy of history.[5] The most famous and influential author to write on this subject in the sixteenth century was Jean Bodin, whose treatise was published several years after that of Patrizi (1566). Most important is Patrizi's *Poetics,* of which he published only two sections (*Della poetica,* 1586), five more remaining in manuscript. This work, which is composed in dialogue form, occupies a special position in the voluminous literature on the subject that was produced in sixteenth-century Italy.[6] For Patrizi carries his anti-Aristotelian bias into a field which had been dominated by Aristotle's *Poetics* for several decades, and which was still to be dominated by it far into the seventeenth and eighteenth century, not to speak of the attempted revival in our own time, often referred to as the Chicago school of criticism. Patrizi's aim was to dethrone Aristotle and to construct another poetics that was partly original and partly based on Plato, an attempt that has not yet been sufficiently studied.

So far we have mentioned only those of Patrizi's Italian works that reflect his literary interests and associations. To them we may add a large number of letters, which have been published only in part. His work as a humanist scholar is represented primarily by his translations from the Greek. The selection of the authors whom he translated is characteristic, for it reflects both his polemical interest in Aristotle and his preference for the Platonic, Neoplatonic, and even pseudo-Platonic tradition. He translated Philoponus's commentary on Aristotle's *Metaphysics* (1583),[7] Proclus's *Theological* and *Physical Elements* (1583), the treatises attributed to Hermes Trismegistus, and the *Chaldaic Oracles* attributed to Zoroaster (1591). There is an unpublished treatise on Pythagorean numbers,[8] and several autograph manuscript excerpts from Greek writers.[9] He also edited in Latin the so-called *Theology of Aristotle* (1591), an apocryphal Arabic work based on Plotinus,[10] and tried to use it as a testimony against the known works of Aristotle, to prove that Aristotle was in agreement with a number of Platonic doctrines. In addition, Patrizi attempted to establish a new sequence of the Platonic dialogues, and one of his major works, the *Discussiones peripateticae* (1571, enlarged 1581), combines a good deal of scholarly spadework, especially a first collection of Aristotle's fragments, with a philosophical critique of Aristotle. In this work he gives a detailed tabulation of all the points on which Plato and Aristotle agree and disagree with each other, and tries to show that Plato is right on all counts. Elsewhere, he tries to prove that Plato agrees on many issues with Catholic doctrine, whereas Aristotle is in conflict with both Plato and the Church.[11] In accepting the *Theology of Aristotle* as an authentic work, Patrizi did not show good judgment, but with his collection of Aristotle's fragments, he became a forerunner of modern Aristotelian scholarship, and this effort may show us that at least in some instances dislike is as much of an incentive for scholarly enterprises as love and enthusiasm usually are.

Patrizi's mathematical interests are represented by a treatise on geometry (*Della nuova geometria,* 1587), and by another on mathematical and physical space (*De rerum natura libri II,* 1587), both of which were later incorporated, apparently in a revised form, in his chief work, the *Nova de universis philosophia,* which appeared in Ferrara in 1591, and again in Venice in 1593. Unpublished are some manuscript drafts of the same work, as well as the defense of his *Nova Philosophia* that he submitted to the Congregation of the Index after 1593.[12]

After speaking so much of Patrizi's role as a philosopher of nature, and his claimed or real originality, we must also give due emphasis to his links with the Platonist tradition. These two sides of his work are by no means incompatible. For in trying to construct a new system of the universe, he was at the same time making use of his favorite sources, and in acknowledging his debt to these sources, he was probably more candid than some of his fellow philosophers in his own time and at other times. Patrizi's Platonist orientation appears from the very titles of some of his writings, and from the content of many more. Platonic is the tendency of his *Poetics* and his *Peripatetic Discussions.* One of his earliest writings (1553), which deals with the various kinds of poetic madness, is based on a Platonic theme, and his treatise on the philosophy of love, although not especially "Platonic" in its content, belongs to a literary tradition that went back to Ficino and was closely associated with the Platonist tradition in the sixteenth century. His interest, too, in the writings attributed to Zoroaster, Hermes, and Pythagoras reflects a tendency of Renaissance Platonism and goes back to Ficino, and through Ficino to Proclus, whom Patrizi had translated. It is in the name of Plato and Platonism that Patrizi argues against Aristotle and prefers the spurious *Theology* to his authentic works. We also learn from one of Patrizi's letters that he became interested in Platonism at an early age when he heard a discourse by a Franciscan friar on Platonic philosophy and read, upon the friar's suggestion, Ficino's *Platonic Theology.*[13]

As we learn from Patrizi's Prefaces, he advocated in the name of the Catholic religion that Plato's philosophy should be taught at the universities instead of Aristotle's, and it was upon his own request and initiative that he was given during his later years a chair of Platonic philosophy, first at Ferrara and then at Rome. This was a rare, if not a unique, instance in which Renaissance Platonism succeeded in penetrating the university teaching of philosophy. Patrizi attained only a part of his aim, for we know for sure that Aristotle continued to be taught along with Plato, by many other professors, both at Ferrara and elsewhere.

In his attempt to make a close comparison between Plato and Aristotle, Patrizi followed a Platonist tradition that can be traced in antiquity from Antiochus of Ascalon and Cicero to Ammonius Saccas and Boethius, and that we find again in the Renaissance, not only in Pico but also in Patrizi's contemporaries Francesco Verino il Secondo and Jacopo Mazzoni. Yet whereas these predecessors had tended to harmonize Plato and Aristotle, Patrizi uses the comparison for an attack on Aristotle, and this anti-Aristotelianism, which is directed not only against the school but against the master himself, distinguishes Patrizi from most other Platonists of antiquity and of the Renaissance, including Ficino.

There seems to be one other distinctive angle in Patrizi's Platonism and in his anti-Aristotelianism. Plato's philosophy gives a very high status and great importance to mathematical knowledge and its objects, and although not all Platonist philosophers have emphasized this particular side of Plato's thought, it is for this reason that Plato has at all times had a great appeal for mathematicians. In a comparison between the philosophies of Plato and Aristotle, such as was attempted by several thinkers of the sixteenth century, it must appear obvious that mathematics, as compared with physics, had a higher status for Plato than it had for Aristotle. It was this very point that played a role in Galileo's admiration for Plato, and we shall see that the problem was of some importance to Patrizi. Whether the attempt to replace the qualitative physics of Aristotle with a quantitative, that is, mathematical, physics was ever really made before Galileo, and whether Plato's authority was used in this connection, is not too certain, and would have to be further explored.[14]

We may add that in his effort to emphasize the harmony between Platonic philosophy and Catholic theology, Patrizi was again following a line similar to that taken by Ficino and other Renaissance Platonists. In turning now to Patrizi's chief philosophical work, we shall see that several of its characteristic ideas show the influence of Plato and his ancient and Renaissance followers, but that the system as a whole has nevertheless an originality and significance of its own.

Patrizi's *Nova de universis philosophia* was published twice during his lifetime, in 1591 and in 1593. It was preceded by several other publications, which were subsequently incorporated in the larger work, and a few drafts and fragments have been preserved in manuscript.[15] Patrizi planned to revise his work, after it had been criticized by ecclesiastic censors, and at least parts of the criticisms and of Patrizi's two writings in defense of the work have been preserved in manuscript, and have been studied and partly published. Yet a detailed comparison between the earlier writings, the manuscripts, and the editions of 1591 and 1593 has never been made, and a critical edition that would illustrate the textual and philosophical evolution of the work would be extremely desirable. I mention these facts, since the work as we read it in the two printed editions shows a certain number of gaps, overlappings, and inconsistencies, on which a study of its textual history might very well throw some further light.[16]

The *Nova de universis philosophia* is divided into four major parts, to which Patrizi gave similar-sounding Greek titles, and which seem to have been composed as separate works before he decided to combine them in a single volume. The first part is entitled *Panaugia,* which we may roughly translate as "All-Splendor," and he seems to have borrowed this unusual word from a passage in Philo of Alexandria.[17] This part is divided into ten books and deals with the physical and metaphysical properties of light. This twofold treatment of light leads to a strange combination between optical observations and metaphysical speculations, and this is justified for Patrizi by the principle that light occupies an intermediary place between divine, incorporeal things and corporeal objects. Following a well-established earlier usage in Latin, he distinguishes between *lux* and *lumen*. The former is the light as it is found in its source, whereas the latter is the light as it is found diffused outside its source (Bk. I). These two aspects of light are linked with each other by the rays that proceed from the source and pass into the surrounding world (Bks. III–IV). In the physical world, light has a special importance as a source of movement and of life.

After discussing the different nature of lucid, transparent, and opaque bodies (Bks. II and V), and touching upon such phenomena as the reflection and refraction of light, and the nature of colors, he ascends from the celestial to the supercelestial light (Bk. VIII). He asserts that outside the visible universe, which is finite and in which the celestial light is mixed with darkness, there is an infinite space filled with pure light, and this he calls the empyrean. This light outside the celestial world is still corporeal, but it has its source in the incorporeal light, which belongs to the incorporeal and divine things, that is, to the souls, intellects, angels, and God (Bk. IX). The ultimate source of this incorporeal light is God Himself (*lux prima*), and from Him proceeds the diffused light (*lumen*), which is found first in His Son, and then in all incorporeal creatures (Bk. X). God is also the ultimate source for the secondary light, which is found in the physical world. Thus light is said to be infinite, and may be considered incorporeal in its source, while it is both incorporeal and corporeal when considered in its state of irradiation, and thus mediates between God and the corporeal world.

The mixture of physical science with metaphysical and theological speculation as its appears in this section is certainly strange for a modern reader, and all we can say to excuse it is that Patrizi lived and wrote at a time when the emancipation of physical science from philosophy had not yet been achieved, and when a similar mixture may be encountered in the work of much greater scientists, for example, in Kepler. As far as Patrizi is concerned, light is one of his basic physical principles, as we shall see, and its prominent and monographic treatment in the first part of his work is thus understandable. Since the other physical principles posited by him do not receive such a full and separate treatment, it seems probable that this section reflects an earlier phase of his thought, and was written at a time when his views on the other principles had not yet been fully developed. When we discuss the other parts of his work, and consider its composition as a whole, we shall see that he treats the incorporeal and the physical world in different sections. Hence he may have felt that the treatise on light had to be placed at the beginning of the entire work, for the very reason that he conceives of light as belonging to both basic parts of reality.

Patrizi's theory of light may also be better understood if we consider it against the background of a long earlier tradition that was known to him at least in some of its phases. In Plato's *Republic,* the sun is called the image of the idea of the good, and this analogy is developed by Plato in great detail.[18] In Plotinus, light and its irradiation became a basic metaphor for the diffusion of goodness and being from their respective sources, and from Plotinus the metaphor found its way into later Neoplatonism, and through St. Augustine and the Areopagite into Christian thought. The metaphor was easily turned into a symbol, and even into a literal ontological relationship, and from this starting point developed the medieval tradition of light metaphysics, which included Grosseteste, and which made its contribution to the development of optics as well as of metaphysics.[19] Marsilio Ficino offered a symbolical and ontological interpretation of the light metaphor that he found in his Neoplatonic sources, and he even composed a special treatise on light, in which he discussed both corporeal and incorporeal light and their relationship.[20] Once more we recognize Patrizi's close connection with the Platonist tradition. We may add that his speculation on light seems to have been continued into the seventeenth century by one of his successors in Ferrara, Tommaso Giannini.[21]

The second part of Patrizi's work is called *Panarchia,* a title that seems to be patterned after *Hierarchia* and might be translated "a series of all principles." This part has twenty-two books, and deals with the hierarchy of being in a fashion that might roughly be called Neoplatonic. Patrizi's prevailing scheme is as follows: the One (also called the one-all, "unomnia," and identified with God), unity, essence, life, intelligence, soul, nature, quality, form, and body (Bk. XI). This scheme reveals the influence of several known sources, but in some details, and as a whole, it is original. The sequence One, intelligence, soul, nature, and body is Plotinian. The separation of unity from the One, and of essence and life from intelligence, goes back to Proclus. The insertion of quality is derived from Ficino.[22] The introduction of form as a separate level of being seems to be an innovation, and may be due to Patrizi's preoccupation with geometry and its status. Unfortunately, we cannot be more specific, because the lower part of the hierarchy is barely sketched in Patrizi's work, and the section as a whole is concerned only with the higher degrees of being.

The Neoplatonic scheme is then further developed with the help of several theological notions. Patrizi deals at length with the attributes of God or the one-all. Unlike Plotinus, Patrizi believes that all things are in God as well as from Him. God has an internal product, namely the unity including plurality, which is identified with the order of ideas, and also with the second person of the Trinity. God's external product is the universe, which includes pure spirits, souls, and bodies. The ideas and the persons of the Trinity are said to emanate from God while staying within Him, whereas the universe is created by God

(Bk. XXII). It is clear from this outline that Patrizi is trying to combine Neoplatonic and Christian notions, and that there remain several inconsistencies and undeveloped details which we cannot discuss any further.

The third part of Patrizi's work consists of only five books and is entitled *Pampsychia,* that is, the theory of the all-soul. In good Neoplatonic fashion, Patrizi treats the soul as intermediary between the spiritual and the corporeal world. How this middle position of the soul is related to the similar position assigned to light in the first section he does not tell us anywhere. He takes over from Lucretius the distinction between *animus* (mind) and *anima* (life-principle),[23] and discusses at length the world soul, which he treats as the animating principle that permeates the entire corporeal universe (Bk. IV). This notion, which the Neoplatonists had inherited from the Stoics, had been treated with reservation by the medieval thinkers, without ever having been clearly condemned. It was reintroduced by Ficino, and enjoyed great popularity with most of the philosophers of nature during the sixteenth century. Patrizi does not treat the individual souls as parts of the world soul, but believes, rather, that their relation to their bodies is analogous to that of the world soul to the universe as a whole. In this he reflects again the position of Plotinus, who had criticized the Stoics for making the individual souls parts of the world soul, thus depriving them of a separate status and of free will.[24]

The fourth and last part of Patrizi's work is by far the most interesting and original. It consists of thirty-two books, and deals with the physical world, as the title *Pancosmia* (the theory of the all-cosmos) indicates. Patrizi introduces four basic principles of the physical world (which he obviously intends to take the place of the four Aristotelian elements): space, light, heat, and humidity.

Patrizi discusses these four principles one by one. Space is for him the first principle of all corporeal things. It consists of a finite space, which is located in the center, the position occupied by the corporeal world, and is therefore called mundane space, and of an infinite external space, which is empty and surrounds the former one on all sides. Space is prior to all bodies, and even to light, and is conceived as an empty receptacle (Bks. I–III). In this notion Patrizi evidently follows Telesio, but he differs from him in several ways. He does not put time on the same level as space, as Telesio had done, but regards it as dependent on both bodies and motion,[25] thus reverting in this respect to the Aristotelian view. On the other hand, he uses the concept of space for the theory of geometry, and in a manner that seems to foreshadow Kant. For he makes a distinction between mathematical and physical space. Mathematical space is pure and contains no bodies, and its minimum is the pure point; whereas physical space is derived from pure space, and contains bodies (Bks. I–III). Bodies, according to Patrizi, are more than three-dimensional forms, since, in addition, they contain resistance. This added factor of resistance seems to reflect a doctrine attributed by several ancient sources to Epicurus, who in this way revised the earlier view of Democritus.[26] In a similar way, Leibniz was to correct Descartes's purely geometrical conception of corporeal nature by the addition of the concept of force.

Having thus defined the difference between mathematical and physical space, Patrizi proceeds to state that mathematics, and especially geometry, is prior to physics, just as pure space is prior to physical bodies, indicating once more his Platonist leanings. Being prior to all bodies, space is even called both a body and incorporeal, and hence the categories that apply to bodies only (again a Plotinian reminiscence[27]) cannot be predicated of space.

In his treatment of number, Patrizi reverts again to the Aristotelian position. The continuum is for him prior to the discretum, and hence geometry is prior to arithmetic (Bk. II). Whereas he regards space as having a real existence of its own, he considers number to be merely a product of thought. This primacy of geometry within mathematics is clearly a Greek heritage. It was to be abandoned only after Descartes had invented analytical geometry, and after modern mathematics had extended the concept of number, and eventually made it continuous.

The second physical principle, which comes after space, is light, the first thing to fill empty space (Bk. IV). At this point, the doctrine of the first section of Patrizi's work, the *Panaugia,* fits into the scheme of the last, although the relationship between the two is not made completely clear. Patrizi then adds two other physical principles: heat, which he considers derived from light, and which he treats as a formal and active principle (Bk. V), and humidity (*fluor*), which is considered a passive and material principle (Bk. VI). The latter is capable of different degrees of density, and accounts for the resistance that characterizes physical bodies in distinction from pure geometrical forms. Heat as an active principle of the physical world seems to be borrowed from Telesio, as had been the notion of empty space (although, for Telesio, space had not been a separate principle of the universe). Humidity takes for Patrizi the place of Telesio's and Aristotle's matter, and the term *fluor,* as well as the insistence on its different degrees of density, evidently reflects certain notions of the pre-Socratic philosophers, notions undoubtedly known to Patrizi from a variety of ancient sources.[28]

The later chapters of the *Pancosmia* contain a discussion of the various parts of the physical universe. This universe consists of three major sections, the empyrean, the aetheric world, and the elementary world. The empyrean is identical with the infinite space that surrounds the celestial world and is filled with nothing but light (Bk. VIII). The aetheric world includes all stars down to the moon. It is finite in extent, and may be called the universe in the more specific sense of the term (Bk. IX). For Patrizi, the stars move freely in the aether. He thus abandons the traditional notion of solid spheres, which had still been retained by Copernicus,[29] and comes in this respect closer to the more modern view represented by Tycho Brahe. The earth remains for Patrizi in the center, and it does not revolve around the sun, but he accepts the daily rotation of the earth around itself (Bk. XXXI). In dealing at some length with the sea and the earth, he discusses a number of meteorological and geographical questions, referring more than once to his own observations. This section contains many details that are of great interest for the history of the sciences (Bks. XXIV–XXXII).

I have tried to present as briefly as possible the general structure and content of Patrizi's chief philosophical work, and I hope both its strength and its weakness have become apparent. The work reflects a forceful attempt at systematizing, but also reveals a number of loopholes and inconsistencies. It shows a mixture of science and speculation, of originality and dependence on the Platonist tradition and on other sources. Yet Patrizi is a vigorous mind, remarkably free of occultism, both learned and acute, and quite unusual in his combination of humanistic and scientific interests. We should not be surprised to find in his work a strange blending of disparate elements, of Platonism with an original philosophy of nature, of ideas that are clearly obsolete (and this includes some of his original ideas) with others that are still valid, or foreshadow those of some illustrious successors (and this includes some of his traditional ideas). Patrizi is a transitional thinker, and this is more or less true of all philosophers of our period.

It is not true that the Renaissance was a period of stagnation, let alone of retrogression, in the fields of science and philosophy, as many medievalists would like to tell us. Even if this were true, we still might be interested in a period that surely made great contributions to learning, literature, and the arts. For I do not think that human achievement should be measured exclusively in terms of the sciences, as it is now fashionable to maintain. Yet the statement made by the medievalists is not true. The fifteenth century transmitted to its successors the entire heritage of the Middle Ages, and added to it the contributions of classical antiquity by making them completely available for the first time.[30] The sixteenth century was thus able to appropriate the results of ancient science in their entirety, and it made the first novel additions to them, especially in mathematics, astronomy, and medicine. Yet when we speak of the origins of modern science, we are thinking primarily of mathematical physics, and this began with Galileo, whose activity includes the last years of the sixteenth century, and who, though in many ways indebted to Renaissance traditions, belongs with the essential part of his work to the seventeenth century and a new age. Modern science, understood in this sense, is not a product of the Renaissance, although it surely had some of its roots in the Renaissance, and especially in the sixteenth century.

The same remarks may be made about modern philosophy. Francis Bacon is in many ways a Renaissance thinker, and his relation to modern science is still transitional and ambiguous. We may regard him with equal right as the last great thinker of the Renaissance and as the prophet and harbinger of modern thought. The real founder of modern philosophy is Descartes, and he begins a new epoch in philosophy because he presupposes the modern science of Galileo and Kepler as a given fact, takes an active part in its further development, and tries to base philosophy, in its method and its subject matter, upon this new science. This attitude has determined, if not completely dominated, the course of modern philosophy up to the present day. In this sense, Renaissance philosophy, including the philosophers of nature, is clearly not modern. Rather, its significance lies in the many ways in which it led up to modern thought (as we have had occasion to observe in several instances, including the case of Patrizi) and in its concepts *per se*. A thinker like Patrizi deserves a good deal of attention both for the intrinsic merit of his original ideas and for the way in which he restates the *philosophia perennis* of Platonism. He shows us once more that a tradition does not live merely by repetition, but by a continuous transformation of its basic ideas. The old heritage is constantly being rethought, adapted, and supplemented in order to incorporate new insights and to solve new problems. The example of Patrizi may show us that it is quite possible to philosophize within a tradition, and to be original at the same time.

8

Bruno

To devote this last chapter to Bruno, and to conclude our survey of Renaissance philosophy with his work, seems appropriate for a number of reasons. Bruno is probably the most famous of the thinkers we have discussed, or at least as well known as Petrarch and Pico. This fame is partly due to the tragedy of his life and death, but no less deserved by his brilliant gifts as a thinker and writer. His vision of the world has a distinctly modern quality, and has impressed and influenced scientists and philosophers throughout the subsequent centuries. At the same time, his work is still entirely a part of the Renaissance, not merely in its date and style but in its premises and problems, whereas such younger contemporaries or successors as Bacon, Galileo, and Descartes belong to the Renaissance with only a part, and perhaps not the most significant part, of their thought and work.

Giordano Bruno was born in Nola in southern Italy in 1548, and entered the Dominican order in Naples at the age of 18. While pursuing theological studies, he also read extensively in the ancient philosophers, and began to entertain serious doubts about some of the teachings of the Catholic Church. When he was in Rome in 1576, these doubts became known to the authorities of his order, and an indictment for heresy was prepared against him. Before he could be arrested, Bruno escaped and began a long and adventurous journey that took him to many parts of Europe. He went first to Noli near Genoa, then to Savona, Turin, Venice, and Padua, and apparently earned his living by private teaching and tutoring, as he did throughout most of his later life until his arrest. From Padua he went to Lyons, and then to Geneva, where he became a Calvinist and met many of the Reformed leaders. Yet soon he turned against Calvinism and went to Toulouse, where he obtained a degree in theology and lectured on Aristotle for two years. Next he went to Paris, where he obtained the favor of Henry III, held some kind of a lectureship, and published his first writings in 1582. He then accompanied the French ambassador, Michel de Castelnaud, Marquis de Mauvissière, to England, and spent the period from 1583 to 1585 in London. He also held a disputation, and gave a few lectures, at Oxford, and antagonized the professors both by his manners and by his polemical attacks. Yet he made friendly contact with Sir Philip Sidney and other educated Englishmen, and his English period is especially noteworthy because he published in London, in Italian, some of his most famous writings.

He returned to Paris with his patron, and held in 1586 in one of the colleges of the university a violent disputation against Aristotle, which caused such an uproar that he decided to leave. He went to Marburg and then to Wittenberg, where he lectured for two years at the university on Aristotle's logic, became a Lutheran, and praised Luther in his farewell address. He then proceeded to Prague and to Helmstedt, where he lectured again at the university, and in 1590 to Frankfurt. His stay in Frankfurt was again important, since it was in this city, which was then, as now, a center of the international book trade, that he published his Latin poems (1591), the most important of his published works after his Italian dialogues.

When he was in Frankfurt, he received and accepted an invitation from Giovanni Mocenigo, a Venetian nobleman. After a short stay in Padua, Bruno joined the household of Mocenigo in Venice as his guest and tutor. Shortly afterwards, Mocenigo denounced him to the Inquisition and had him arrested in 1592. Bruno tried to retract, but in January 1593 he was taken to Rome, kept in prison, and subjected to a trial that lasted for many years. After initial hesitations, he firmly refused to recant his philosophical opinions. Finally, in February 1600, he was sentenced to death and burned alive in the Campo di Fiori, where a monument was erected to him during the last century.

Bruno's dreadful end has rightly shocked his contemporaries and posterity. His firm conduct during the trial deserves our highest respect, and goes a long way to balance his human weaknesses, which are all too obvious. The idea that a man should be punished and executed for holding opinions considered wrong by his religious or political authorities is intolerable for any thoughtful person who takes human dignity and liberty seriously, although the deplorable treatment given to Bruno, and the wrong idea underlying it, was by no means peculiar to Bruno's church or to his century, as some historians would have us believe. His death made of Bruno a martyr, not so much of modern science, as was thought for a long time, but rather of his convictions and of philosophical liberty. The records of his trial have not been completely preserved, but several relevant documents have been published, and some very important ones have come to light quite recently, from which the nature and content of the charges made against him have become much clearer than before. It is now quite evident that Bruno's acceptance of the Copernican system constituted but one out of a very large number of accusations, which included a long series of philosophical and theological opinions as well as many specific instances of alleged blasphemy and violations of Church discipline.[1]

Bruno's extant writings are rather numerous and diverse in content. His Italian works, which were all published during his lifetime, include a comedy and several satirical treatises, in addition to his philosophical dialogues, which we shall discuss later. His style is lively and exuberant, and at times quite baroque and obscure. His more numerous Latin writings, some of which were published only in the last century whereas others have come to light quite recently, include several important philosophical poems and treatises, as well as a number of works that reflect his subsidiary interests: mathematics and magic, the art of memory, and the so-called Lullian art.

The art of memory, which grew out of a part of ancient rhetoric, was a subject much cultivated in the Middle Ages and the Renaissance, and there are many treatises dealing with this subject, which scholars have just recently begun to study, and which probably deserve much further exploration.[2] These efforts to devise systems for strengthening a person's memory had a very great practical importance in a period when scholars and men of affairs could not rely as heavily as nowadays on the help of indexes and reference works, and when the ready mastery of knowledge and information was considered a necessary criterion of competence, not only in speeches and disputations but also in many professional activities.

The Lullian art, named after its inventor, the fourteenth-century Catalan philosopher Ramon Lull, was a general scheme of knowledge based on a number of simple terms and propositions, and it was Lull's claim that through appropriate methods of combination this art would lead to the discovery and demonstration of all other knowledge. The method was illustrated by the use of letters, figures, and other symbols, which represented the basic concepts and their combinations.[3] The Lullian art attracted the interest of many thinkers and scholars down to Leibniz, and it is obviously, at least in its claims if not in its achievements, a forerunner of modern symbolic logic. For Bruno, the art of memory and the Lullian art were not merely the subjects of his intellectual curiosity, but also a means of livelihood, for he seems to have instructed his private pupils mainly in these two arts. This side of Bruno's work is less well known, and a detailed study of it has been attempted only in recent years.

Bruno's thought shows many traits of genuine originality, yet at the same time he is indebted to a variety of sources. In spite of his double polemic against the grammarians and the scholastics, he owed much to his humanist education as well as to his Aristotelian and scholastic training. His doctrine of heroic love, which forms the center of his famous *Eroici furori*, is heavily indebted to Ficino, and it has been recently shown that this work belongs to the literary and intellectual tradition of Platonist love treatises, which occupied a rather large place in sixteenth-century thought and literature.[4] In his metaphysics, Bruno was strongly influenced by Plotinus and Cusanus, whereas his cosmology is based on Lucretius and Copernicus.

Many historians have discovered serious inconsistencies in Bruno's thought, and some scholars have tried to account for them on chronological grounds, assuming that his philosophical thought underwent a certain development. Without excluding such a development, I am inclined to think that from the time of his Italian dialogues his basic position remained unchanged, and that a few ambiguities, oscillations, and logical difficulties are inherent in this very position. At least on one important point that is unclear in Bruno's published writings, a recently discovered document from his last years throws a good deal of light.[5]

Some of Bruno's chief ethical doctrines are contained in his famous *Eroici furori*, a group of dialogues in which the recital and interpretation of a series of poems by Bruno and others, and the explanation of a number of symbolic mottos and devices, occupy a large place, interrupting as well as enlivening the presentation of the chief philosophical ideas. In a free variation upon the common theme of Platonizing love treatises, Bruno opposes heroic love and frenzy to vulgar love. Heroic love has a divine object, and leads the soul in a gradual ascent from the sense world through intelligible objects toward God.[6] The union with God, which is the ultimate and infinite goal of our will and intellect, cannot be attained during the present life. Hence heroic love is for the philosopher a continuous torment.[7] But it derives an inherent nobility and dignity from its ultimate goal, which will be reached after death. It is this emphasis on the suffering which accompanies the unfulfilled heroic love during the present life that distinguishes Bruno's theory from that of most previous writers on the subject, and this may also explain why he chose to call the higher love heroic rather than divine.

A more central aspect of Bruno's thought is expressed in his dialogue *De la causa, principio e uno,* in which some of his basic metaphysical ideas are discussed. He starts from the fundamental notion that God must be conceived as a substance, and His effects as accidents.[8] This is a complete reversal of the traditional Aristotelian notion of substance, according to which the term substance had always been applied to particular sense objects, whereas their permanent or passing attributes had been called accidents. For Bruno, there remains only one substance, namely God, and all particular objects, far from being substances, become accidents, that is, passing manifestations of that single substance. This notion resembles in many ways that of Spinoza, and it has often been asserted that Spinoza owed this basic conception to Bruno, although there seems to be no tangible evidence that Spinoza was familiar with Bruno's thought or writings.

In order to know God, Bruno continues, we must know His image, nature. In pursuing this task, Bruno proceeds to apply to the universe the four causes that in Aristotle and his school had merely served as contributing factors in the attempt to understand particular objects or phenomena. Developing some occasional remarks in Aristotle, Bruno divides the four causes into two groups, one of which he calls causes in the stricter sense of the word, and the other, principles. Form and matter are principles because they are intrinsic to their effect, whereas efficient and final cause are external to their effect.[9] He then identifies the efficient cause of the world with the universal intellect, which is the highest faculty of the world soul.[10] He is drawing here on Plotinian notions, and there is no evidence that he is identifying the world soul or its intellect with God. On the contrary, he explicitly distinguishes this world intellect from the divine intellect, and states

Bruno

that it contains in itself all forms and species of nature, just as our intellect contains in itself all its concepts. Working as an internal artist, this world intellect produces out of matter all material forms, which are images derived from its own internal species.[11] The final cause of the world, on the other hand, is nothing but its own perfection.[12]

The principles, that is, internal constituents, of nature are form and matter.[13] They correspond in name to Aristotle's formal and material cause, but are in fact conceived along Plotinian lines. Bruno asserts that the form coincides to a certain extent with the soul, insofar as every form is produced by a soul. For all things are animated by the world soul, and all matter is everywhere permeated by soul and spirit. Thus it may be said that the world soul is the constituent formal principle of the world, just as matter is its constituent material principle. The world is thus a perpetual spiritual substance that merely appears in different forms.

In this way, form and matter are both perpetual substances and principles, and mutually determine each other, whereas the bodies composed of form and matter are perishable, and must be regarded not as substances but as accidents.[14] Bruno thus seems to conceive of particular things as resulting from a changing interpenetration of two universal principles, and in this suggestive and original view also lies the basic difficulty of his philosophy.

In God, Bruno goes on to say, form and matter, actuality and potentiality, coincide.[15] In what appears to be an important modification of his previous statements, he says that also in the universe there is only one principle, which is both formal and material, and thus the universe, considered in its substance, is only one.[16] This one principle, taken with its two aspects, is said to constitute both all corporeal and all incorporeal beings.[17] Bruno here seems to follow the so-called universal hylemorphism of Avicebron, who, too, composes all incorporeal beings of form and matter.[18] This statement reveals still another basic ambiguity, which Bruno had inherited from Cusanus and other earlier philosophers, and which he never completely overcomes, at least in this work. That is, in speaking about nature and the universe, Bruno seems to think primarily in terms of the physical universe, but at the same time he includes in the universe all incorporeal beings except God. Speaking of matter, he insists that it is not merely negative, but contains in itself all forms, thus taking up a theory of Averroes, and departing from both Aristotle and Plotinus, who had thought of matter as pure potentiality.[19]

Identifying the universe with the substance that comprises both form and matter, Bruno states that the universe is one and infinite, that it is being, true and one, whereas all particular things are mere accidents and subject to destruction.[20] There is no plurality of substances in the world, but merely a plurality of manifestations of a single substance. The plurality of things is only apparent and belongs to the surface grasped by our senses, whereas our mind grasps, beyond this surface, the one substance in which all apparent contrasts coincide.[21] This substance is true and good, it is both matter and form, and in it actuality and potentiality are no longer different from each other. In such formulas the distinction between the universe and God seems to disappear, but in one important passage Bruno differentiates between the physical universe known by the philosophers and the archetypal universe believed in by the theologians.[22]

He thus presents us with an impressive and original vision of reality, but if we compare the various statements contained in the dialogue, a few basic ambiguities remain. Form and matter are clearly universal principles for Bruno, but he treats them sometimes as distinct and sometimes as identical, or rather as two aspects of the same principle. The physical and the metaphysical universe are sometimes identified, and sometimes quite clearly distinguished. Finally, the universe is sometimes treated as an image of God, and as distinct from Him, whereas at times this distinction tends to disappear.

Students of Bruno have tried to cope with these difficulties in a variety of ways. Some have emphasized one set of statements over the other, thus making of Bruno either a Platonist metaphysician or an outright pantheist. Those who have been willing to admit the ambiguities present in his work have often considered the extreme pantheist position to be his true position, and the dualist statements to be concessions made to popular opinion or potential censors or critics. Others have regarded pantheism as the logical consequence of his position, which he came to adopt gradually, the dualist statements representing a mere residual of his earlier views. This last opinion seems to be the soundest of the ones we have cited. However, I am more inclined to think that Bruno had a vision that was not completely expressible in terms of these antitheses, and that he was quite willing to accept the dilemma, that is, both horns of it, as a paradox and an approximation, without wishing to be pushed into a more extreme position. It is no doubt true that in comparison with his favorite sources, Plotinus and Cusanus, Bruno goes much further in the direction of a pantheistic or immanentistic conception. Yet I doubt very much that he wanted to be an extreme pantheist or naturalist. In one of his latest statements, he tries to show that individual minds are particular manifestations of the universal mind, just as particular bodies are manifestations of universal matter.[23] This statement is a welcome addition to his other writings, in which this particular doctrine is not so clearly stated. It also shows that his position was closer to Cusanus and to the dualistic passages in his dialogues than many interpreters have been willing to admit.

No less interesting and historically significant than Bruno's metaphysics is his conception of the physical universe as we find it developed in his dialogue *De l'infinito, universo e mondi*. In this work, Bruno restates the Copernican system of the universe, and gives it for the first time a philosophical meaning.[24] His chief emphasis is on the infinity of the universe as a whole, as against the innumerable finite

worlds that are contained in it. This distinction between the universe
and the worlds is borrowed from Lucretius, as is the notion of the
infinity of the universe, which is not found in Copernicus at all.[25] We
now know that in the sixteenth century the infinity of the physical
universe was asserted by Thomas Digges, prior to Bruno, but it is not
certain that Bruno was familiar with the writings of this predecessor.[26] We might also compare the view of Patrizi, who assumed an
infinite external void surrounding our finite world. For Bruno, there
are many such worlds as ours, and the universe outside our world is
not a void. Moreover, unlike Patrizi, he conceives our world or solar
system according to the system of Copernicus. He further insists that
this infinity of the universe cannot be perceived by the senses, but is
disclosed by the judgment of reason,[27] thus reverting to Democritus
from the sensationalism of the Epicureans and Telesio.

The infinite universe is for Bruno the image of an infinite God.[28]
In this context, at least, he clearly distinguishes between God and the
universe, and his position may be compared with that of Cusanus. Yet
whereas Cusanus reserves true infinity for God alone, Bruno uses the
relation between the universe and God as an argument for the infinity
of the former. Since God is infinite, also the universe must be infinite,
although in a different sense.[29]

As for Patrizi and others, the stars are no longer attached to rigid
spheres, but move freely in the infinite space. Yet in accordance with
the Neoplatonic tradition, and with a view adopted by most medieval
Aristotelians, Bruno assigns the cause for the motion of the stars to
their internal principles or souls.[30] The earth is also in motion, and
may hence be considered as one of the stars.[31] Only the universe as a
whole is at rest, whereas all particular worlds contained in it are in
motion. The universe as a whole has no absolute center and no absolute direction; that is, we cannot talk of an upward or a downward
direction in an absolute sense. Gravity and lightness have merely a
relative meaning with reference to the parts of the universe toward

which a given body is moving.[32] This view of Bruno's may be characterized as half-Aristotelian. That is, in his denial of an absolute center,
Bruno repeats a formula of Cusanus, interpreting it in a Lucretian
sense. In his denial of an absolute direction, he follows the atomists
against Aristotle; but in retaining a relative direction, and, above all,
in retaining the distinction between gravity and lightness, he is still
under the spell of Aristotelian physics.

The individual stars, Bruno argues, are subject to continual change
through the influx and efflux of atoms, but persist through some internal or external force.[33] The notion of influx and efflux is again
based on atomism, and the notion that the stars are subject to change
is another important departure from Aristotelian cosmology, in
which the celestial objects, as distinct from the sublunar ones, are considered unchangeable and incorruptible. Yet the internal force seems
to be a Neoplatonic rather than an atomistic conception. Bruno knows
that the fixed stars are at varying distances from us, and thus discards
the traditional notion of a single sphere of fixed stars.[34] He thinks that
the entire universe is filled with aether even in the so-called empty
spaces between the stars.[35] All stars in the universe are divided into
two basic groups, which he calls suns and earths. The prevailing element of the former is fire, of the latter, water.[36] Our earth is like a star,
and when seen from the outside, it shines like the other stars.[37] Bruno
also assumes that the various worlds outside our own are inhabited.[38]
He denies the existence of elementary spheres, thus rejecting another
basic conception of traditional Aristotelian cosmology, and calls the
notion of a hierarchy of nature a mere product of the imagination.[39]

Bruno's cosmology is quite suggestive, and it anticipates in a number of ways the conception of the universe as it was to be developed
by modern physics and astronomy. He is not only the first major
philosopher who adopted the Copernican system, but also one of the
first thinkers who boldly discarded such time-honored notions as the
radical distinction between things celestial and earthly, and the hier-

archical view of nature. Being aware of the novelty of his view, he does not spare Aristotle or his followers, whom he pursues with a series of polemical attacks. The fact that Bruno still retains some residuals of Aristotelian physics should not be exaggerated, and it should have been expected in any case. On the other hand, it has been rightly stressed that he was a forerunner, but not a founder, of modern science and philosophy. He was unaware of the role that mathematics and experimental observation were to play in modern science, and did not develop a precise method by which his assertions might have been tested or demonstrated. His merit and his limitation lie in the fact that, through his intuition and vision, he anticipated a number of ideas that resemble those which later centuries were to adopt and to develop on the basis of much more solid evidence. Yet the more we are inclined to extol the role of imagination in the sciences, alongside that of empirical observation and logical deduction, the more we should appreciate the contribution made by such thinkers as Bruno.

The extent of Bruno's influence during the following centuries is hard to estimate. His condemnation and terrible end made it impossible for any Catholic scholar to read or cite him overtly, and even in Protestant countries his works seem to have had a rather limited circulation for a long time. Yet Galileo could have read Bruno long before the latter was condemned, and the resemblance between certain passages in Galileo and Bruno that deal with the place of the earth in the universe is so great that it may not be incidental after all. I am also inclined to see a connection between Bruno and Spinoza, for the conception of the relation between God and particular things as substance and accidents is too similar and too unusual to be a mere coincidence. Aside from many other differences, it was quite natural for Spinoza to replace Bruno's two basic principles, form (or soul) and matter, which have a Neoplatonic, and if you wish an Aristotelian, origin, with the attributes of thought and extension, which are derived from the system of Descartes. I cannot discuss the question whether the theory of monads, as developed in some of Bruno's Latin writings, may have had an influence on Leibniz.

We have now completed this rather brief treatment of eight selected thinkers of the Renaissance. All these men happen to be Italians, and they represent but a very small number out of the large series of philosophical writers who were active in Italy alone during the three centuries or so we have been trying to cover. I hope the selection has been representative, not only of Italian, but also of European, thought during the Renaissance period. Many thinkers whom we have not discussed held different opinions, or different combinations of opinions. Yet I believe the general intellectual climate in which they worked, and the chief problems with which they were concerned, were roughly the same; for the schools we have tried to describe—humanism, Platonism, Aristotelianism, and the new philosophy of nature—are more or less inclusive of the thinkers of the period, both in Italy and in other European countries. If I have not spoken of Erasmus or More, Vives or Montaigne, among many others, it does not mean that I consider them less important. I had to make a narrow choice, and this choice was determined by the limits of my own scholarly interests, curiosity, and knowledge.

If we try to assess, at the conclusion of our survey, the intellectual heritage that Renaissance thought left to subsequent centuries including our own, the answer cannot be given in a single sentence, and it is wise to break it up, and to talk separately of the different trends we have been discussing. Renaissance humanism was a complex movement that had its impact on scholarship and literature as well as on moral thought and philosophy. As a scholarly movement, it is responsible for the pervasive classicism and the rise of classical (or humanistic) education that began with the fifteenth century and persisted almost until the early years of our century. The humanists also began to formulate and practice the methods and techniques of philological and historical scholarship, and these methods have since been developed and refined, and have been applied to a variety of other subjects, but have not fundamentally changed. As historical and literary scholars, even when we are historians of philosophy or science, we must consider the humanists as our professional predecessors. In literature, humanism was primarily associated with a reform of Neo-Latin literature, which led to a greater classical purity in language, style, and prosody, and to a revival of many ancient genres. This effort is often underestimated because it has by now become obsolete, but it had a considerable importance down to the eighteenth century. More indirect, but from our point of view more important, was the impact of humanism on the various vernacular literatures. Its effect was felt in the introduction of classical themes and classical genres, and in the quest for greater neatness of linguistic and stylistic expression.

In the field of philosophy, we owe it to the humanists if we have easy access to ancient philosophers besides Aristotle, Cicero, Seneca, Boethius, and Proclus, and if we are able to read Plato, Plotinus, Epictetus, Epicurus, Lucretius, Sextus Empiricus, or even much of Alexander of Aphrodisias. We are also indebted to them for the fact that we are no longer bound by the scholastic argument (or, at least, were not bound by it until a few years ago), and that we are permitted to express our thoughts not only in commentaries and questions, but in papers and essays, books and monographs.

In other words, in scholarship, literature, and philosophy, Renaissance humanism brought to the Western world a large body of secular learning and literature that was neither religious nor scientific or professional, and that, without being either anti-religious or anti-scientific, came to occupy a large and independent place, alongside theology and the professional disciplines, in education, writing and thinking. Humanist learning, much more than the rather meager liberal arts course of the Middle Ages, is the fountainhead of what we

praise as the humanities, something to which we attribute a broadening effect, and which should not merely be a matter of a so-called
general education or a leisure occupation, but one of the integral elements of our life and outlook. I find that much lip service is being
paid to the humanities in academic circles, but that they are notably
absent from our public discussion, which, when it rises above purely
practical matters, seems to leave us with nothing but the bleak alternative between science and religion. I am also dismayed when I hear
and read that our heritage, aside from our political institutions, consists solely of the scientific method and the Judaeo-Christian tradition,
as if we owed nothing to Greek philosophy, or to other aspects of ancient, medieval, or early modern civilization, or as if the "Judaeo-
Christian tradition" itself, a very complex and diversified tradition,
did not derive many of its elements from Greek philosophy, as most
thoughtful and informed students of religion and theology are quite
ready to admit. When I am confronted with such current problems,
I begin to wonder whether our humanistic heritage and our historical and philological studies are perhaps more·than just scholarly pursuits, and contain serious philosophical implications whose importance it is high time to develop, and to present to the public before
the frightening impoverishment of our educational and cultural system has gone too far.

Renaissance Platonism is in some of its aspects closely allied with
humanism. It is responsible for the easy access we have to the works
of Plato and other Platonist writers. It revived or kept alive the Platonist tradition, which has as much right as any other in Western
thought to be considered a *philosophia perennis,* and it represents
within the history of Platonism one of its more important phases. In
its general orientation and in some of its specific ideas, Renaissance
Platonism is closely linked with the rationalist and idealist tradition
in modern philosophy, and its influence may be recognized in many
of the later phases of this tradition. This school of thought is still very

much alive in Europe, and although it has been somewhat out of fashion in the United States for the last generation or so, it may still regain some favor and vitality in the future.

Renaissance Aristotelianism, which we have studied in the case of Pomponazzi, represents a very different attitude, but one that has been no less important in modern thought. It worked toward a clearer separation between philosophy and theology, and without arriving at a purely naturalistic or anti-religious position, it paved the way for such later movements in Western thought.

Finally, the Renaissance philosophers of nature, in their brilliant and partly original attempts to formulate new systems, are the forerunners of the speculative side of modern philosophy, which has been disciplined, but by no means extinguished, by the steady and successful progress of the natural and other sciences.

I hope our hasty survey may also have suggested, if not proven, what I tried to indicate at its very beginning. That is, the philosophical thought of the Renaissance goes a long way to provide an intellectual background for the art, literature, and other cultural manifestations of the period. Actually, a good deal of work has been done during the last few decades, on the part of historians of art and literature, to discover the philosophical sources behind the iconography of Renaissance art, and behind the imagery and thought in Renaissance poetry. These investigations are far from being completed, and the solidity of their results varies greatly from case to case. Yet some of the examples presented, and the conclusions reached, are convincing, and others at least promising. We have learned to see Botticelli and Michelangelo, and to read Marlowe and even Shakespeare, with greater precision because we now understand that some of their images and thoughts are not merely vague ornaments, but specific expressions of ideas then current; and our enjoyment of their work does not seem to have suffered from this insight. For the historian of philosophy who tries to read and interpret the writings of Renaissance thinkers, the service he may thus be doing his fellow historians of literature and art is certainly an incentive, and almost a duty.

Another important aspect is the role of Renaissance philosophy within the history of Western thought. The philosophical importance of the great thinkers of antiquity and of the seventeenth century has never been questioned, and the significance of the medieval philosophers of the twelfth, thirteenth, and early fourteenth centuries has been increasingly recognized during the last fifty or eighty years. In a sense, the thought of the thirteenth century and that of the seventeenth are comparable because each of them represents a compact intellectual achievement with a great unity and solidity of style. The thought of the intervening period lacks such unity and compactness. It is a period of fermentation, in which many new sources were assimilated, and many new ideas, or new combinations of old ideas, were proposed and tried out. Yet if we wish to understand why the philosophy of the seventeenth century was as different from that of the thirteenth as it was, and why it was possible to pass from one to the other, we must study the intellectual development of the intervening centuries. It is Renaissance thought, through its diversified and even chaotic efforts, that brought about the gradual disintegration of medieval philosophy and prepared the way for the rise of modern philosophy; it is Renaissance thought, therefore, that accounts for the difference between the one century and the other, in sources and literary style, in terminology and problems, if not in methods and solutions. For the student of philosophy who also has a scholarly curiosity about the history of philosophy, this development offers special attractions: the subject is not yet very much explored, and the opportunity to discover new texts, to read even printed texts for the first time after centuries, and to replace traditional but erroneous formulas and interpretations with more correct ones that can be documented from the sources, has a fascination all of its own.

Apart from the influence Renaissance philosophy may have exerted on the thought of later centuries, and on the civilization of its own time, and apart from the place it may occupy in the historical evolution of Western philosophy, I should like to stress the intrinsic interest that the study of this subject, and the study of the whole history of philosophy, may hold for the student of philosophy. It is justified not merely by the broadening effect that this travel in time has upon our mind, as has the travel to other countries, offering us different alternatives in addition to the familiar ones of current thought, and helping us to see our own accustomed modes of thinking in their proper perspective. It is justified, too, because any genuine system of thought, just as any serious work of art, represents a specific and unique essence that deserves to be contemplated and absorbed before we can analyze and criticize it. Such a thought has an eternal quality, and perhaps Pico was right after all in claiming that every philosophy represents an aspect, or contains a part, of that universal truth at which we all aim, and of which each of us is permitted to see but one part, or at best, a few aspects.

Appendix

The Medieval Antecedents of
Renaissance Humanism

A discussion of the medieval antecedents or background of the Renaissance, or any Renaissance phenomenon, might easily seem to give aid and comfort to those medievalists who have been taking the line that every aspect traditionally associated with the Renaissance is also found in the Middle Ages, or at least that everything of any worth in the Renaissance is basically medieval. I do not think that this line is tenable. If we wish to insist that there was no sudden break between the Middle Ages and the Renaissance, but a kind of continuity, we must also understand that continuity is not the same thing as stability, but may involve a good deal of gradual change and cumulative innovation. If this were not so, we could not possibly understand why the world looked so different in 1600 from its appearance in 1300.

This change is due partly to the change of succeeding generations (a factor usually forgotten by those theorists who enquire about the causes of historical change), and in part to a number of important events that are too well known to require special comment, such as the invention of printing, the discovery of America, and the Reformation. There was a constant change of style and fashion that gives not only to the Renaissance period as a whole, but also to many shorter periods within it, their peculiar physiognomy. And although each European country and region made its own specific contributions to the common civilization of the whole medieval and Renaissance

147

period, and although this civilization continued to be in many ways universal or international, it is a significant fact that during the Middle Ages, as again in the seventeenth and eighteenth centuries, most of the intellectual and cultural movements of the West had their center of irradiation in France, whereas in the period between 1350 and 1600 a similar position of leadership was held by Italy. Finally, if we look for the medieval antecedents of certain significant Renaissance developments, we must be prepared to find them not in the most famous and most frequently studied aspects of medieval intellectual history, but in certain minor and secondary aspects that seem to be rather unimportant within the context of their own time, but acquire a special significance as the modest beginnings of ideas, and modes of thinking, that came to full maturity only during the subsequent period— just as the water that rises with the crest of the wave does not come from the crest of the preceding wave, but rather from the intervening trough. Thus it is easy to contrast medieval scholasticism and Renaissance humanism, as has been done so often, but I do not think that it is at all possible to derive the latter from the former. If we seek medieval sources and antecedents for Renaissance humanism, we must try to find something like medieval humanism. For this purpose, it is not enough to give the term humanism some arbitrary or Pickwickian meaning, and to call the great scholastic theologian St. Thomas Aquinas a medieval humanist, or a Christian humanist, or a true humanist, as several distinguished historians have recently done. We must rather try to understand, not what humanism should have been if it were to look good by modern standards, but what Renaissance humanism really was, and then ask the perfectly legitimate question whether this specific phenomenon, Renaissance humanism, had any antecedents in the Middle Ages, and what they were.

To understand Renaissance humanism, or to give a satisfactory definition of it, is not so easy as we may wish. Of course, we should begin by discarding the contemporary notion of humanism, which indicates, in a rather hazy fashion, any kind of emphasis on human values and human problems. Much of the recent discussion on Renaissance humanism has suffered from the conscious or unconscious use of the modern overtones of the term, and the result has been a good deal of confusion. Yet even if we avoid this trap, the difficulty remains great enough. In recent years the controversy over the meaning of Renaissance humanism has been almost as complex and confusing as that over the Renaissance itself. Some historians have associated Renaissance humanism with certain political, theological, and philosophical ideas, and speak of civic humanism, or of Christian or religious humanism, or extend the term to include the entire body of secular thought and philosophy produced during the Renaissance period. Others, following a tradition that goes back to the nineteenth century, have considered Renaissance humanism primarily for its contributions to classical scholarship or to the development of literature. To complicate matters even further, Renaissance humanism has been associated with paganism, or with Protestantism, or with Catholicism, and consequently it has been debated whether humanism was superseded by the Protestant and Catholic Reformation, or changed its complexion as a result of these events, or continued to live in its original form.

Most of these views, though incompatible with one another and subject to criticism, seem to contain some nucleus of truth. I cannot go into a full discussion of them here, but shall try instead to present my own view of the matter. I have tried to find a formula that would do justice to most, if not all, aspects and achievements of Renaissance humanism, and at the same time come as close as possible to what the Renaissance itself understood by the term humanist. For the term humanism was coined in the early nineteenth century, but the term humanist (*humanista*) goes back to the late fifteenth century and was in common use during the sixteenth. From the documents of the period it appears beyond any doubt that the later Renaissance understood by a humanist a teacher or student of the humanities, of the *studia hu-*

manitatis. For the term *studia humanitatis* is even older than the term humanist, which was derived from it. It appears in the writings of ancient Roman authors such as Cicero and Gellius, and was taken over from them by fourteenth-century scholars such as Salutati (see p. 170, n. 24). In this ancient usage, the humanities stood for a kind of liberal education, that is, for a literary education worthy of a gentleman.

In the fifteenth century, the term *studia humanitatis* acquired a more precise and technical meaning, and appears in university and school documents as well as in classification schemes for libraries. The *studia humanitatis* were then defined as comprising five subjects: grammar, rhetoric, poetry, history, and moral philosophy. In other words, in the language of the Renaissance, a humanist was a professional representative of these disciplines, and we should try to understand Renaissance humanism primarily in terms of the professional ideals, intellectual interests, and literary productions of the humanists. It is true that many Renaissance humanists cherished the ideal of a universally educated person, and the humanist Vives designed an encyclopaedia of learning on humanist rather than scholastic principles. It is also true that many humanists, or scholars with a humanist training, had strong interests in other subjects besides the humanities, and made significant contributions to these subjects. Yet it is important to realize that the professional home territory of the humanists was a well-defined and limited cycle of studies, which included a certain group of disciplines and excluded others.

For the Renaissance had inherited from the later Middle Ages a highly articulated and specialized body of learning. The days of the seven liberal arts when the sum total of secular learning could be easily mastered by any competent student had been over for a long time. Their place had been taken, after the tremendous increase of learning in the eleventh and twelfth centuries, the introduction of large numbers of scientific and philosophical texts translated from the Arabic and Greek, and the rise of advanced instruction in the universities during the thirteenth century, by a number of specialized disciplines that were no longer mastered by the same persons, and hence developed each its own distinct tradition: theology, Roman and canon law, medicine, mathematics, astronomy and astrology, logic and natural philosophy, and finally grammar and rhetoric.

This articulation of learning that characterized the later Middle Ages still provided the backbone of instruction during the Renaissance, although it underwent a number of changes and additions. In other words, if we want to understand the history of those learned disciplines that did not belong to the humanities, we must study Renaissance theology, jurisprudence, medicine, mathematics, logic, and natural philosophy against the background of the medieval traditions in these fields, even though all these disciplines underwent some significant changes during the Renaissance, partly under the influence of humanism, and partly for other reasons. Thus the Aristotelian logic and natural philosophy of the Renaissance is linked with the scholastic Aristotelianism of the Middle Ages, and the same is true of the other disciplines just mentioned. Vice versa, if we look for the continuation of medieval Aristotelian logic or physics in the Renaissance, we have to explore Renaissance Aristotelianism, something that has not yet been done to a sufficient extent. When historians of science make the statement that Renaissance humanism retarded the progress of science by a century or two, the remark is completely beside the point. It is like saying that the progress of science in the twentieth century is being impeded by the literary critics or by the existentialist philosophers. The Renaissance, like the later Middle Ages, was a period of diversified and often competing intellectual interests and traditions, and we cannot properly understand any thinker or movement unless we place them firmly where they belong within this system of intellectual coordinates.

Thus I should like to take it for established that Renaissance humanism was often incidentally, but never primarily or consistently, concerned with theology or speculative philosophy, with law or the natural sciences, and that therefore it cannot be closely associated with the medieval traditions of these other disciplines. It belonged basically to another school or department of learning. We must try to understand what the subject matter of the humanities was, and then we can ask the question what its medieval antecedents were.

We have listed the names of the five humanistic disciplines, but it might be good to explain the specific meanings of the terms as then understood, since they often differ from the ordinary usage of our own time. The teaching of the first subject, grammar, included, as it does now, the formal rules governing the use of the language; but, in addition, it involved the elements of Latin that the schoolboy had to learn as a preliminary tool for all other studies, since Latin continued to serve as the language, not only of the Church, but also of scholarship and university instruction, and of international conversation and correspondence. Hence it was of vital importance for any professional person to be able not only to read Latin, but to write and speak it. Moreover, ever since classical antiquity it had been the task of the grammar teacher to read with his students the standard Roman poets and prose writers. With the fourteenth century, the study of poetry begins to be separated from that of grammar, and grammar tends to be confined to a more elementary level. The study of poetry clearly had a twofold purpose, as we learn from a number of documents. The student was taught to read and understand the classical Latin poets, and at the same time he learned to write Latin poetry. The two tasks were almost inseparable, for the ability to write Latin verse was acquired and developed through a close study and imitation of the ancient Latin models. In other words, neither aspect of the humanist study of poetry was concerned with vernacular poetry, and the humanist concept of poetry and the poet was far removed from the ideas to which Romantic and modern theories of aesthetics and literary criticism have accustomed us. When Petrarch was crowned as a poet on the

Capitol, the event must be understood in terms of this humanist concept of poetry, as we may learn from the oration Petrarch gave on that
occasion, and from the diploma bestowed on him. For the humanists,
the concept of poetry, as we have tried to explain it, was of great importance. During the fifteenth century, before the term humanist had
been coined, humanists were usually known by the name of poets, although many of them would hardly deserve the label by modern standards. This notion also may help us to understand why the defense of
poetry, one of the favorite topics of early humanist literature, involved
a defense of humanist learning as a whole.

No less important than poetry was the humanist study of rhetoric or
oratory, and again the humanists were very often identified as orators,
or as both poets and orators, before the term humanist had come into
use. In a sense, the study of rhetoric was the study of prose literature, as
distinct from the study of poetry, and consisted in an analogous fashion in the reading and interpretation of the ancient Latin prose writers,
and in the exercise and practice of Latin prose composition through
the imitation of ancient models. In the study of rhetoric, heavy emphasis was placed upon two branches of prose literature that had a much
broader practical importance and application than any of the poetic
genres ever possessed: the letter and the speech.

In the Renaissance as in other periods, the letter was not merely a vehicle of personal communication, but also a literary genre that served
a variety of other purposes: news reports, political manifestos or mes-
sages, short treatises on scholarly, philosophical, or other learned subjects—all were cast in the form of letters. The humanist was a man
trained to write well, and when he did not choose to become a school
or university teacher of his subject, the most common and lucrative
career open to him was to become the chancellor of a republic or city,
or the secretary of a prince or other prominent person. In such positions, it was his chief task to act as a ghost writer for private or official
letters, and his services were highly valued, since he composed these

Appendix

letters in the style that the taste of the time demanded, and thus helped to maintain the cultural and social prestige of his patron.

Of almost equal practical importance was the literary genre of the oration. Historians have often said that the humanists composed their speeches to indulge their personal vanity, and thus forced their audiences to listen unwillingly to their long-winded discourses. This view is quite mistaken, although I should not wish to deny that the humanist tended to be rather vain. The documents show that in the Renaissance, and especially in fifteenth-century Italy, public oratory was a favorite form of entertainment, comparable to the role played at the same time or in other times by musical or theatrical performances, or recitals of poetry. Moreover, Italian society had developed a variety of occasions on which a public speech came to be demanded as a necessary element of the program. A speech was required for the funeral or wedding of prominent persons, for a number of public ceremonies such as the inauguration of a magistrate or the welcome given to a distinguished foreign visitor, and for academic exercises such as the opening of the school year or a course of lectures, and the conferring of a degree, to mention but a few of the most common genres. No wonder that the extant literature of humanist speeches is so large, and yet it obviously represents but a small portion of what was actually composed and delivered. Again, the humanist was the person trained to speak well, and was in demand as a writer of speeches that were to be delivered either by himself or by others. Hence the humanist chancellors and secretaries were supposed to compose speeches as well as letters for their patrons or employers, and since it was customary for an ambassador to begin his mission with a public speech in the name of his government, we often find a humanist acting, if not as the chief ambassador, at least as one of the subordinate members of the mission.

The fourth subject among the *studia humanitatis,* history, had traditionally been linked with oratory, and during the Renaissance, too, it was usually taught as a part of oratory. The ancient historians were

154

Appendix

among the favorite prose authors studied in the schools, and again the practical purpose of imitation was linked with the study of the texts. It was customary for princes, governments, and cities to commission a humanist to write their history, and the job of the official historiographer was often combined with that of the chancellor or the teacher of rhetoric. After the middle of the fifteenth century, this practice was imitated by foreign princes, and we find a number of Italian humanists serving foreign kings as their official biographers or historians, and sometimes also as their secretaries.

The fifth and last branch of the *studia humanitatis,* moral philosophy, is in a sense the most important, and the only one that belongs to the domain of philosophy. It is to their interest in moral philosophy that the humanists primarily owe their place in the history of philosophy, apart from their work as scholars and writers. For much of the work of the humanists had nothing to do with philosophy, and much of the philosophical thought of the Renaissance falls outside the area of humanism, as we have tried to define it. Hence I am reluctant to identify humanism with the philosophy of the Renaissance, as some other scholars have tended to do. The claim that they were moral philosophers was made by the humanists since the time of Petrarch, and some of them actually occupied university chairs of moral philosophy, along with those of rhetoric and poetry.

When the humanists were prompted by the attacks of narrow-minded theologians to defend their studies, they insisted upon their concern with moral and human problems, and claimed to provide a moral as well as an intellectual training for the young, a claim that is also expressed in the ambitious term *studia humanitatis.* Hence it should not surprise us to find a strong moralistic note in the humanist study of history and of ancient literature, and to notice that the humanists' orations and other writings are studded with moral maxims. Yet the main expression of this aspect of humanism is found in the large body of moral treatises and dialogues that deal with a great va-

155

riety of topics. There are treatises on happiness or the highest good, echoing the ethical systems of ancient philosophers, and on particular virtues, vices, and passions. Other works deal with the duties of a prince, a magistrate, or a citizen; of particular professions; and of women and married life. Other favorite topics are the education of children; the origin of nobility; the relative merits of the various arts, sciences, and professions, and of the active and contemplative life; the dignity of man; and the relation between fortune, fate, and free will.

The views presented in these treatises are rarely original, often interesting, and always historically important. In accordance with the interests of the humanists, the concern for erudition and literary elegance was at least as great as for the formulation of precise ideas. Personal opinions and observations of contemporary life are intermingled with repetitions or restatements of ancient philosophical theories. With reference to ancient thought, the tendency was rather eclectic, and the humanists borrowed more or less freely from many authors and schools. Yet there are also significant attempts at reviving and adapting the positions of specific authors or schools. Even Aristotle, whom the humanists took over from the scholastics but placed into a different context, had his admirers and defenders, whereas the moral views of Plato and the Neoplatonists, and of the Stoics, Epicureans, and Sceptics, were more widely discussed and more frequently endorsed than had been possible in the preceding centuries. Thus humanist scholarship, if it did not produce a body of systematic ideas, had a fermenting effect in the field of moral thought, and supplied a large mass of secular ideas that were to influence the following centuries, and were by no means eliminated by the Reformation, as is so often believed.

So far we have tried to follow the cycle of the *studia humanitatis,* and to circumscribe in this fashion the intellectual range of Renaissance humanism as we find it expressed in the professional activities and literary compositions of the humanists. I hope it has become evident that the result of these activities represents a peculiar and unique combination of intellectual interests that left its impact upon the entire period, even outside the area of the humanist studies. The concern for moral and human problems, the literary ideal of eloquence and poetry, the scholarly study of the classical writers who served as indispensable models of imitation, all these factors were combined in the work of the humanists in such a way that the separate threads are often very hard to disentangle. We have discussed the humanists' classical studies primarily with reference to the Latin classics. We must now add a few words about the role and development of Greek studies during the Renaissance.

The place of Greek in Renaissance humanism is somewhat different from that of Latin, and some of the conflicting opinions about the classical scholarship of the Renaissance are due to the attention scholars have paid either to the Latin or to the Greek scholarship of the period. Latin as a living language of scholarship and literature was inherited, after all, from the medieval period, during which the study of Latin grammar and the reading of at least some Roman classical authors had never been interrupted since ancient times. Consequently, the innovations brought about by the humanists in the field of Latin studies may seem to be less radical, although it would be wrong to underestimate their vast contributions: the attempt to reform the written use of Latin, to cleanse it from "barbaric" usages, and to bring it back as close as possible to ancient classical practice; the great increase in the number of ancient Roman texts that were now read and studied, commented upon, copied and printed; and the vast production of a Neo-Latin poetry and prose literature, in a great variety of genres, that was extremely successful and influential in its own time and down to the eighteenth century.

In the field of Greek studies, these medieval precedents were almost completely absent. Throughout the medieval centuries, there was no continuity of Greek instruction anywhere in the West; Greek books were almost non-existent in Western libraries, except for those regions in southern Italy and Sicily where Greek continued to be spoken; the number of scholars who learned Greek was small, and the texts that were translated from Greek into Latin between the eleventh and the early fourteenth century were either theological, or limited to the same fields that had characterized the Arabic reception of Greek culture, namely the sciences and pseudo-sciences, Aristotelian philosophy, and some Neoplatonic philosophy. In the field of Greek studies, therefore, the humanist contribution was much more incisive than in Latin, and it made itself felt only during what we might call the second phase of Renaissance humanism. Its result was the introduction of Greek instruction into the Western universities and secondary schools, and the gradual diffusion, study, translation, and interpretation of the entire body of ancient Greek literature. Western scholars now became acquainted, not only with Greek scientific writings or with Aristotle, but also with the other Greek philosophers, with the poets, orators, and historians, and even with a large part of Greek patristic literature. The Middle Ages surely knew Vergil and Ovid, Cicero and Aristotle; but we are indebted to Renaissance humanism for the fact that we also know Lucretius and Tacitus, Homer and Sophocles, Plato and Plotinus.

Yet important as these contributions to Greek scholarship were, they did not have the scope and influence of the innovations in Latin studies. Even in the Renaissance, fewer people knew Greek than Latin, and fewer still knew Greek as well as Latin. Consequently, the Greek authors were more widely diffused in Latin translations or bilingual (Greek and Latin) editions than in their original texts as such. Moreover, the cases when Western humanists attempted to write in Greek were extremely rare, and the practical need for Greek correspondence largely disappeared with the fall of Constantinople in 1453. The study of Greek language and literature thus had from the very beginning a much more purely scholarly character than that of Latin; it lacked the broad practical and literary significance that the study of Latin continued to possess for several more centuries.

In the light of what I have tried to show, it will be easily understood when I say that the literature produced by the humanists is full of significant ideas, but that there is no single philosophical or theological idea, let alone any set of ideas, that is common to all Renaissance humanists. Whenever we encounter an interesting opinion in the work of a humanist, we must be prepared to find the very opposite idea defended by another humanist, or even by the same humanist in some other passage. Moreover, a large area of humanist literature is not relevant to the history of philosophy at all: for example, the humanists' poetry and historiography, their translations and commentaries, and much of their oratory. Hence all recent attempts to define civic humanism or Christian humanism may be valid for a specific group of humanists, but cannot help us to understand the humanist movement as a whole. For a good deal of humanist literature is not civic, but despotic, or unrelated to political thought; and a good deal is not Christian, but unrelated to the subject matter of religion. The study of the humanities had become professionalized, as jurisprudence, medicine, mathematics, logic, and natural philosophy had been for some time. Except for those humanist writings that deal explicitly with religious or theological subjects, humanist literature is Christian only in the sense that it was written by Christians—just as Thomas Aquinas is not a Christian philosopher, as Gilson wants us to think, but a Christian theologian and an Aristotelian philosopher. In making these statements, I do not wish to imply that Renaissance humanism was in any sense pagan, or anti-Christian, as it has often been called. It did not oppose religion or theology on its own ground; rather, it created a large body of secular learning, literature, and thought that coexisted with theology and religion.

Having described Renaissance humanism as objectively as I can, I shall now try to answer the question what its medieval antecedents were. In part, the answer is implied in what I have said, but I shall attempt to formulate it more explicitly. In my opinion, there are basically three medieval traditions that contributed to the rise of Renaissance humanism: the *ars dictaminis* of medieval Italy; the study of grammar, poetry, and the classical Roman authors as it had been cultivated in the schools of medieval France; and the study of classical Greek language, literature, and philosophy as it had been pursued in the Byzantine Empire.

The *ars dictaminis* was the theory and practice of letter-writing, which occupied an important place in medieval education and learning, at least after the middle of the eleventh century. Just as the notary was trained with the help of rules and models to compose contracts and other legal documents in a proper form, so the secretaries or chancellors of popes and bishops, of princes and cities, were trained to compose state and business letters with the help of rules adapted from ancient rhetoric, and models that were either fictitious or based on famous contemporary examples. The practical side of the matter was taken care of by classifying the letters according to their content or purpose, but there also developed a concern for stylistic standards of diction and composition. This concern extended, too, to private and personal correspondence, probably because illiteracy was widespread even among the upper classes, and the trained "dictator" had many occasions to supply upon request, and probably for pay, a love letter or a personal message. On account of its great practical importance, the *ars dictaminis* tended in many schools to take the place of rhetoric, an ancient subject that was much broader in scope, but also more abstract and theoretical.

The development of the *ars dictaminis* can be traced in many European countries, and a large body of literature connected with it has been preserved that originated in Germany, Spain, and especially France. However, in this field as well as in medicine and law, medieval Italy acquired and maintained a position of exceptional importance, which may be credited to the proximity of the papal Curia, to the rise of the city republics, and to the links between the *dictamen* and the flourishing study of law. In the thirteenth century, the *dictamen* was extended in scope and importance by the addition of another related study, the *ars arengandi*. The purpose of this study was to teach the composition of public speeches, again with the help of both rules and models. This technical development of secular eloquence was peculiar to Italy, and it was obviously connected with the public life of the city republics, and with the developing customs and institutions of the various governments and university communities. From the thirteenth century on, there appears an increasing body of speech models and of speech rules, and in this literature, which was at first scanty and humble, we find already most of the genres that were to characterize the oratory of the humanists: the funeral and the wedding speech, the ambassador's speech, the opening lecture, and the graduation speech. This literary development begins some time before the rise of Renaissance humanism, and some of the oratory even continues for a while in its medieval pattern after the appearance of the humanistic movement. Yet I find it necessary to conclude that the humanists, at least in some important aspects of their work, were the successors of the medieval *dictatores*. They inherited the same professional positions as chancellors and secretaries that their predecessors had held, and they inherited the two literary genres that were connected with these professions, and that continued to be of great practical importance: the letter and the speech.

Nevertheless, the letters and speeches of the medieval chancellors, though composed for similar occasions and purposes, were quite different in style and diction from those of the humanists, and they lacked almost entirely what was to be the special pride of the humanists: their classical elegance and erudition. If we want to find the medieval sources for the humanist study of classical Latin literature, we have to look in another direction. The elementary study of Latin

161

grammar, along with the reading of a few classical writers, constituted, of course, the irreducible core of medieval school instruction, in
Italy and elsewhere. However, the more advanced study of the Latin
poets and prose writers, and the effort to imitate them in the composition of verse and prose, had been a specialty of the Northern schools
ever since Carolingian times, and especially of the French cathedral
schools. Up to the twelfth and even to the thirteenth century, the
school documents, library catalogues, commentaries on Latin classical
authors, and exercises in Latin poetry—in other words, the entire body
of our evidence—points in the same Northern direction. Yet with the
rise of scholasticism and of the University of Paris in the thirteenth
century, classical and literary studies began to decline in France.

At the very end of the thirteenth century, they begin to appear in
Italy, where up to then they had not flourished very much. From that
time on, Italy produced without interruption an ever-increasing body
of classical manuscripts and commentaries, and of Latin poetry and
prose inspired by the imitation of classical models. At the same time,
the teaching of poetry and of the Roman classical writers entered more
and more firmly into the curriculum of the Italian universities, and
took an ever-increasing share in secondary education. When this study
of poetry, newly imported from France, was combined with, and
grafted upon, the medieval Italian tradition of formal rhetoric, letter-
writing, and speech-making, Renaissance humanism in many of its
characteristic features appeared on the scene. This happened very early
in the fourteenth century, if not before, with Albertino Mussato in
Padua and Giovanni del Virgilio in Bologna. Petrarch was not the
father of humanism, nor the first humanist, but merely the first great
representative of a movement that had begun at least one generation
before his time.

Before Renaissance humanism attained its full stature, one more factor was to be added: the study of Greek. During the fourteenth century, most Italian humanists knew little or no Greek, and there was

hardly any teaching of Greek. Neither Petrarch nor Salutati knew Greek to speak of, and their learning is entirely based on Latin sources, or on Greek writings available in Latin translations. A first modest beginning was made around 1360, when Boccaccio arranged for Leontius Pilatus to give a few public lessons of Greek and to translate Homer into Latin. More important were the activities of the distinguished Byzantine scholar Manuel Chrysoloras, who taught at Florence and other Italian universities at the very end of the fourteenth century. After 1400, Greek instruction was more or less continuously available at many Italian universities, and after the middle of the fifteenth century, the study of Greek began to spread to the other Western countries. The earliest teachers of Greek were either the Byzantine scholars who had begun to come to Italy long before the fall of Constantinople, but whose number greatly increased after that disastrous event, or Italian scholars who had studied in Constantinople under Byzantine professors, as was the case of Guarino and Filelfo. All these scholars carried with them to the West entire libraries of Greek classical manuscripts, and helped to establish in the various Western schools centers of Greek learning that were to last for many centuries, sometimes to the present day.

Thus we many say without exaggeration that the Greek learning of the Renaissance humanists, which constituted such an important part of their contribution, was to some extent a heritage of the Byzantine Middle Ages. For in the Greek East there had been a more or less continuous tradition of Greek classical learning all through the Middle Ages. Whereas the spoken language moved as far away from ancient Greek as the Romance languages departed from Latin, classical Greek continued to be taught, read, and written. Homer, Plato, and other classical authors were copied, read, and commented upon, and thus preserved. The impact of this tradition on Renaissance learning in the West has not yet been sufficiently explored. Yet the first Greek grammars published for Western students were written by Byzantine scholars, or by Italian scholars trained in Constantinople. The selection and sequence of the Greek authors read in the schools and printed for students seems to reflect Byzantine practice. And the range of the Byzantine curriculum, in which Aristotle was studied along with Plato and the poets, and philosophy along with grammar and rhetoric (to the comparative neglect of the study of logic and natural philosophy), resembles the cycle of the *studia humanitatis* rather than the full curriculum of the medieval and Renaissance universities in the West.

I have tried to show, as briefly as possible, that the medieval antecedents of Renaissance humanism are not to be found in the traditions of scholastic philosophy and theology, where some historians have tried to find them, but rather in three other traditions that occupy a much more marginal place in the customary picture of medieval civilization: Italian practical rhetoric, French grammar and poetry, and Byzantine Greek learning. Each of these three traditions probably deserves greater attention and emphasis in medieval studies than it has sometimes received.

However, I do not wish to give the impression that Renaissance humanism, because it was indebted to these medieval antecedents, was nothing but medieval *dictamen* or French grammar or Byzantine learning. Even when we are concerned with the different phases of a single tradition, the later phases always contain new and different features not entirely reducible to their precedents—a fact that is easily forgotten on account of the tendency of most modern historians to study only the first beginnings of a development, and to ignore its continuation and later phases. In our particular case, the very fact that three different currents came to be merged will suggest that the resulting stream was much bigger and richer than its tributaries and consequently quite different from them.

These contributing sources do account to some extent for the general pattern of Renaissance humanism, but they do not account for the actual wealth and quality of its literary production, for the specific impact of the various classical forms and ideas that were circulated in its wake, or for the new ideas that arose and developed within this general framework. They do not account for the high standing and prestige the *studia humanitatis* attained during the Renaissance period, or for the manifold influences it had on all aspects of Renaissance civilization, on the arts and literature, philosophy, the sciences and all other branches of learning, religion and theology, moral and political thought and practice. Yet these sources, in conjunction, do explain the general framework within which Renaissance humanism developed; they even account for some of its limitations, such as its failure to overthrow and replace, to the great surprise of many historians, the elaborate structure of scholasticism and university learning. For humanism merely supplemented and modified the medieval traditions of the disciplines outside the humanities, and it is only in this sense that humanism marked a new phase in the history of theology and jurisprudence, speculative philosophy, and the natural sciences.

Notes

Notes

CHAPTER I. *Petrarch*

1. Petrarch, *Le traité De sui ipsius et multorum ignorantia,* ed. L. M. Capelli (Paris, 1906), p. 77; translated by H. Nachod in E. Cassirer *et al.,* eds., *The Renaissance Philosophy of Man* (Chicago, 1948), p. 113. Jerome, "Epistola ad Eustochium," in his *Epistolae,* Pt. 1, no. 22, sect. 30 (ed. I. Hilberg, Vienna, 1910, p. 190).

2. *Secretum,* Bk. II (Petrarch, *Prose,* ed. G. Martellotti *et al.,* Milan and Naples, 1955, p. 122).

3. *Ibid.* (ed. Martellotti, p. 98).

4. "philosophie principem," ed. Capelli, p. 72 (tr. Nachod, p. 107).

5. "A maioribus Plato, Aristotiles laudatur a pluribus," ed. Capelli, p. 75 (tr. Nachod, p. 111). Cf. Petrarch, *Rerum Memorandarum Libri,* Bk. I, ch. 25, sect. 12 (ed. G. Billanovich, Florence, 1943, p. 28): "alios fortassis a pluribus, Platonem certe a melioribus laudatum."

6. *Trionfo della fama,* ch. III, lines 4–7:

> Volsimi da man manca e vidi Plato
> Che'n quella schiera andò più presso al segno
> Al qual aggiunge cui dal cielo è dato;
> Aristotele poi, pien d'alto ingegno.

For a variant version of this poem (lines 7–9), see R. Weiss, *Un inedito Petrarchesco* (Rome, 1950), p. 55:

> Ivi vidi colui che pose idea
> Ne la mente divina, e chi di questo
> E d'altre cose seco contendea.

7. Dante, *Inferno,* IV, 131–35:

> Vidi 'l maestro di color che sanno
> Seder tra filosofica famiglia.
> Tutti lo miran, tutti onor li fanno:
> Quivi vid'io Socrate e Platone,
> Che 'nnanzi alli altri più presso li stanno.

Petrarch's imitation and modification of these lines of Dante seems conscious. For a

169

Notes

comparison of the cited passages in Dante and Petrarch, see also G. Di Napoli, *L'immortalità dell'anima nel Rinascimento* (Turin, 1963), p. 62.

8. ed. Capelli, p. 67 (tr. Nachod, p. 102). Cf. *Rer. Mem.*, Bk. II, ch. 31 (ed. Billanovich, pp. 64–65).

9. ed. Capelli, pp. 71–72 (tr. Nachod, p. 107).

10. *Ibid.*, p. 77 (tr. Nachod, p. 113).

11. *Ibid.*, p. 78 (tr. Nachod, p. 115).

12. Petrarch, *Epistolae Rerum Familiarium*, Bk. VI, no. 2 (*Le Familiari,* ed. V. Rossi and U. Bosco, Florence, 1933–42, II, 55–60, at p. 55).

13. *Ibid.*, Bk. XVII, no. 1 (ed. Rossi and Bosco, III, 221–30, at p. 224).

14. *Ibid.*, Bk. IV, no. 1 (ed. Martellotti, pp. 830–44, at p. 840; tr. Nachod, p. 44; ed. Rossi and Bosco, I, 153–61, at p. 159).

15. *Rer. Mem.*, Bk. I, ch. 19, sect. 4 (ed. Billanovich, p. 19): "velut in confinio duorum populorum constitutus ac simul ante retroque prospiciens." Cf. T. E. Mommsen, *Medieval and Renaissance Studies* (ed. E. F. Rice, Ithaca, N.Y., 1959), p. 128.

16. "sola videndi insignem loci altitudinem cupiditate ductus," ed. Martellotti, p. 830 (tr. Nachod, p. 36).

17. L. Thorndike, "Renaissance or Prenaissance?," *Journal of the History of Ideas,* IV (1943), 65–74, at pp. 71–72.

18. *Secretum,* Bk. II (ed. Martellotti, pp. 106–28).

19. *Ibid.* (ed. Martellotti, p. 106): "aliquid licet falsi dulcoris immixtum est . . . atra quadam cum voluptate."

20. E. H. Wilkins, "On Petrarch's Accidia and His Adamantine Chains," *Speculum,* XXXVII (1962), 589–94; S. Wenzel, "Petrarch's *Accidia*," *Studies in the Renaissance,* VIII (1961), 36–48; K. Heitmann, *Fortuna und Virtus: Eine Studie zu Petrarcas Lebensweisheit* (Cologne and Graz, 1958), pp. 102–4 (who cites other passages, but fails to mention the crucial passage from the *Secretum*).

21. ed. Martellotti, p. 840 (tr. Nachod, p. 44); cf. Augustine, *Confessions,* Bk. X, ch. 8.

22. *Ibid.*; cf. Seneca, *Epistolae morales,* VIII, 5. The Seneca passage is not identified by Rossi (I, 159), or by E. Bianchi (who is responsible for this section of the *Prose*), but by Nachod. See also G. A. Levi, "Pensiero classico e pensiero cristiano nel Petrarca," *Atene e Roma,* XXXIX (1937), 77–101, at p. 86.

23. ed. Capelli, pp. 24–25 (tr. Nachod, pp. 58–59).

24. Cicero, *Pro Murena,* 29, 61; *Pro Archia,* 1, 3; cf. *De Re Publica,* I, 17, 28. Gellius, *Noctes Atticae,* XIII, 17; C. Salutati, *Epistolario,* ed. F. Novati, Vol. IV, Pt. 1 (Rome, 1905), p. 216: "connexa sunt humanitatis studia" (I am indebted for this reference to Prof. Charles Trinkaus). Cf. Cicero, *Pro Archia,* 1, 2: "omnes artes quae ad humanitatem pertinent habent quoddam commune vinculum et quasi cognatione quadam inter se continentur." See also Salutati, *Epistolario,* ed. F. Novati, Vol. I (Rome, 1891), pp. 179, 229, 248; Vol. III (Rome, 1896), pp. 330, 517, 599; Vol. IV, Pt. 1, pp. 119, 159. Cf. A. von Martin, *Coluccio Salutati und das humanistische Lebensideal* (Leipzig and

Notes

Berlin, 1916), pp. 106 and 108. See also Leonardo Bruni's Preface to his translation of St. Basil's letter on the reading of pagan authors in his *Humanistisch-Philosophische Schriften* (ed. H. Baron, Leipzig and Berlin, 1928, p. 100).

25. ed. Capelli, p. 90 (tr. Nachod, p. 126).
26. *Ibid.*, p. 45 (tr. Nachod, p. 80).
27. *Ibid.*, p. 70 (tr. Nachod, pp. 105-6).
28. *Ibid.*, pp. 78-79 (tr. Nachod, p. 115).

CHAPTER 2. V*alla*

1. B. L. Ullman, *The Origin and Development of Humanistic Script* (Rome, 1960); J. Wardrop, *The Script of Humanism* (Oxford, 1963). Wardrop's book discusses only certain late phases of the script.

2. P. O. Kristeller, "The European Diffusion of Italian Humanism," *Italica,* XXXIX (1962), 1-20.

3. J. E. Sandys (*A History of Classical Scholarship,* Vol. II, Cambridge, 1908, p. 89) mentions, without source, a Latin translation of Thucydides by Leonardo Bruni, but so far as I know, no such translation ever existed.

4. E. Garin, ed., *Prosatori latini del Quattrocento* (Milan, 1952), p. 600.

5. Boethius, *De consolatione philosophiae,* V, 3-4.

6. Valla, *De libero arbitrio,* ed. Maria Anfossi (Florence, 1934), pp. 38-53; ed. Garin, pp. 552-64; translated by C. Trinkaus in E. Cassirer *et al.,* eds., *The Renaissance Philosophy of Man,* pp. 174-82.

7. ". . . il n'étoit pas moins Philosophe, qu'Humaniste," *Essais de Théodicée,* sect. 405.

8. ed. Anfossi, pp. 7-10; ed. Garin, pp. 524-26; tr. Trinkaus, pp. 155-56.

9. Valla, *Opera omnia* (Basel, 1540, and Turin, 1962), pp. 896-999. See Maristella De Panizza Bové (Mrs. Lorch), "Le tre redazioni del *De voluptate* del Valla," *Giornale storico della letteratura italiana,* CXXI (1943), 1-22, and "Le tre versioni del *De vero bono* del Valla," *Rinascimento,* VI (1956), 349-64.

10. *Opera omnia,* p. 977 (Bk. III, ch. 9): "Nam utramvis consequi possumus, utramque non possumus. Quae sunt inter se contraria, ut coelum et terra, anima et corpus."

11. *Ibid.*, p. 985 (chs. 20-21).

12. *Ibid.*, pp. 966-67 (*De voluptate,* Bk. III, ch. 2); pp. 665-67 (*Dialecticae Disputationes,* Bk. I, ch. 10).

13. *Ibid.*, pp. 896-97.

14. Epicureanism was defended in a letter by Cosimo Raimondi (who died in 1435); see the text in E. Garin, ed., *Filosofi italiani del Quattrocento* (Florence, 1942), pp. 134-48. For Epicurean influences on Ficino, see P. O. Kristeller, *Il pensiero filosofico di Marsilio Ficino* (Florence, 1953), p. 14; Ficino, *Opera omnia* (Basel, 1576, and Turin, 1959), pp. 1009-10 (*De voluptate*); P. O. Kristeller, ed., *Supplementum Ficinianum* (Florence, 1937), II, 81-87.

15. Valla, *Opera omnia*, p. 897.

16. *Ibid.*, p. 978 (ch. 11); cf. p. 980 (ch. 14).

17. *Ibid.*, p. 907 (Bk. I, ch. 10).

18. *Ibid.*

19. *Ibid.*, p. 960 (Bk. II, ch. 39).

20. *Ibid.*, pp. 997–98.

21. *Ibid.*, p. 651 (Bk. I, ch. 3); pp. 684–85 (ch. 17); p. 707 (Bk. 2, ch. 10); pp. 708–9 (ch. 11); pp. 714–15 (ch. 16).

22. *Ibid.*, pp. 693–94.

23. Walter J. Ong, *Ramus: Method, and the Decay of Dialogue* (Cambridge, Mass., 1958). See also Neal W. Gilbert, *Renaissance Concepts of Method* (New York, 1960).

CHAPTER 3. *Ficino*

1. Ficino, *Opera omnia*, p. 119; P. O. Kristeller, *Il pensiero filosofico di Marsilio Ficino*, Florence, 1953, p. 102 (*The Philosophy of Marsilio Ficino*, New York, 1943, p. 106).

2. *Opera omnia*, p. 121; Kristeller, *Il pensiero*, p. 118 (*The Philosophy*, p. 120).

3. Kristeller, *Il pensiero*, pp. 238–39 (*The Philosophy*, pp. 224–25), and the passages cited there.

4. *Ibid.*, pp. 289–96 (pp. 270–76).

5. *Ibid.*, pp. 311–25 (pp. 289–303).

6. *Opera omnia*, pp. 872 and 1537; Kristeller, *Il pensiero*, p. 20 (*The Philosophy*, p. 29).

7. For a recent treatment of the doctrine of immortality in Renaissance thought, see G. Di Napoli, *L'immortalità dell'anima nel Rinascimento* (Turin, 1963).

8. Kristeller, *Il pensiero*, pp. 358–78 (*The Philosophy*, pp. 331–48).

9. *Ibid.*, pp. 282–89, 296–310 (pp. 263–70, 276–88). See also the studies by Robb, Festugière, Jayne, and John Nelson cited in the Bibliography.

10. Kristeller, *Il pensiero*, pp. 342–45 (*The Philosophy*, pp. 316–19).

11. *Ibid.*, pp. 346–49 (pp. 320–23).

12. *Ibid.*, pp. 16–20 (pp. 25–29).

13. Steuco's work was reprinted several times in the sixteenth century. It should be noted that his conception of the perennial philosophy includes the Aristotelian and the Hebrew and Christian traditions, and this view puts him closer to Pico than to Ficino.

14. A. M. J. Festugière, *La philosophie de l'amour de Marsile Ficin et son influence sur la littérature française au XVIᵉ siècle* (Paris, 1941); W. Moench, *Die italienische Platonrenaissance und ihre Bedeutung fuer Frankreichs Literatur und Geistesgeschichte* (Berlin, 1936).

15. Matthias Meier, *Descartes und die Renaissance* (Muenster, 1914).

16. Kristeller, *Il pensiero*, pp. 110, 160 (*The Philosophy*, pp. 112–13, 152).

17. Ch. 9 (ed. J. Shawcross, Oxford, 1907, I, 94; cf. the note on p. 241). For a different judgment by the philologist Lobeck, see below, ch. 4, note 19.

Notes

1. For the text of Pico's letter to Ermolao, see E. Garin, ed., *Prosatori latini del Quattrocento* (Milan, 1952), pp. 804–23 (who also gives Ermolao's reply, pp. 844–63). For an English version of the letters of Pico, Ermolao, and Melanchthon, see Q. Breen, "Giovanni Pico della Mirandola on the Conflict of Philosophy and Rhetoric," *Journal of the History of Ideas,* XIII (1952), 384–426.

2. Breen, *loc. cit.*

3. Pico, *Opera* (Basel, 1572), pp. 63–113 (*Conclusiones*).

4. Pico, *De hominis dignitate, Heptaplus, De ente et uno, e Scritti vari,* ed. E. Garin (Florence, 1942), pp. 138–62; *Apologia,* in *Opera,* pp. 117–24; see also the early draft of the *Oration* in E. Garin, *La cultura filosofica del Rinascimento italiano* (Florence, 1961), pp. 238–40.

5. Joseph L. Blau, *The Christian Interpretation of the Cabala in the Renaissance* (New York, 1944); F. Secret, "Pico della Mirandola e gli inizi della Cabala cristiana," *Convivium,* n.s., XXV (1957), 31–47; F. Secret, *Le Zóhar chez les Chrétiens de la Renaissance* (Paris, 1958); G. Scholem, "Zur Geschichte der Anfaenge der christlichen Kabbala," in *Essays Presented to Leo Baeck* (London, 1954), pp. 158–93; F. Secret, *Les Kabbalistes Chrétiens de la Renaissance* (Paris, 1964).

6. R. Klibansky, "Plato's *Parmenides* in the Middle Ages and the Renaissance," *Mediaeval and Renaissance Studies,* Vol. I, Pt. 2 (1943), pp. 281–330.

7. *De ente et uno,* chs. 4–5 and 8–9 (Pico, *De hominis dignitate,* ed. Garin, pp. 400–422 and 426–38).

8. *Opera,* pp. 256–312.

9. Salutati, *De laboribus Herculis,* ed. B. L. Ullman, 2 vols. (Zurich, 1951).

10. P. O. Kristeller, ed., *Supplementum Ficinianum* (Florence, 1937), I, 80–82.

11. Pico, *De hominis dignitate,* ed. Garin, pp. 546, 556, 581. Cf. Aristotle, *Metaphysics,* I 3, 983 b 27–32; III 4, 1000 a 9–19; XII 6, 1071 b 26–27.

12. ed. Garin, pp. 104–6 (tr. Elizabeth L. Forbes in E. Cassirer *et al.,* eds., *The Renaissance Philosophy of Man,* pp. 224–25).

13. ed. Garin, pp. 266–86, 300–304.

14. Pico, *Disputationes adversus Astrologiam,* Bk. III, chs. 1, 5, and 24 (ed. Garin, Vol. I, Florence, 1946, pp. 178, 210, and 386). See E. Cassirer, "Giovanni Pico della Mirandola," *Journal of the History of Ideas,* III (1942), 123–44, 319–46.

15. Kepler, *Harmonia mundi,* Bk. IV, ch. 7, in his *Gesammelte Schriften,* ed. M. Caspar, Vol. VI, Munich, 1940, p. 266; see also p. 285. I am indebted for these references to Prof. Edward Rosen.

16. Bk. III, ch. 27 (ed. Garin, I, 416). See E. Cassirer, *Individuum und Kosmos in der Philosophie der Renaissance* (Leipzig and Berlin, 1927, reprinted Darmstadt, 1962), pp. 124–26.

17. Ch. 5 (ed. Garin, I, 406–22).

18. Letter to Aldus (1490): "philosophia veritatem quaerit, theologia invenit, religio possidet" (*Opera,* p. 359).

Notes

19. Chr. A. Lobeck, *Aglaophamus* (Koenigsberg, 1829), I, 407.
20. *Noctes Atticae*, XIII, 17: "quod vulgus existimat . . . ; non vulgo dicitur . . ."

CHAPTER 5. *Pomponazzi*

1. F. Edward Cranz, "Alexander Aphrodisiensis," in P. O. Kristeller, ed., *Catalogus Translationum et Commentariorum* (Washington, D.C., 1960), pp. 77–135; F. E. Cranz, "The Prefaces to the Greek Editions and Latin Translations of Alexander of Aphrodisias, 1450 to 1575," *Proceedings of the American Philosophical Society*, CII (1958), 510–46.
2. Pomponazzi, *De fato*, ed. R. Lemay (Lugano, 1957), p. 262.
3. Ch. 12 (*De naturalium effectuum causis sive de incantationibus*, Basel, 1556, pp. 267–69; also in *Opera*, Basel, 1567, pp. 248–51).
4. ed. Lemay, p. 453.
5. Pomponazzi, *De immortalitate animae*, ed. G. Morra (Bologna, 1954), p. 36; tr. W. H. Hay in E. Cassirer *et al.*, eds., *The Renaissance Philosophy of Man*, p. 281.
6. *Ibid.*, pp. 48–68 (tr. Hay, pp. 286–97).
7. *Ibid.*, p. 82 (tr. Hay, pp. 302–3).
8. *Ibid.*, pp. 232–38 (tr. Hay, pp. 377–81).
9. *Ibid.*, p. 168 (tr. Hay, p. 345).
10. *Ibid.*, pp. 184–96 (tr. Hay, pp. 353–59). For the distinction of speculative, practical, and productive (although not applied to the intellect), see Aristotle, *Topics*, VI 6, 145 a 15–16; *Metaphysics*, VI 1, 1025 b 25. For the theoretical and practical intellect, see *De anima*, III 10, 433 a 14–15.
11. ed. Morra, pp. 200–204 (tr. Hay, pp. 361–63).
12. *Ibid.*, pp. 224–26 (tr. Hay, pp. 373–75).
13. See F. Garasse, *La doctrine curieuse des beaux esprits de ce temps* (Paris, 1624), p. 1010; P. O. Kristeller, "El mito del ateísmo renacentista y la tradición francesa del librepensamiento," *Notas y Estudios de Filosofía*, IV (Tucumán, 1953), 1–14.
14. P. Bayle, *Dictionnaire historique et critique*, XII (Paris, 1820), pp. 226–44.
15. J. Presser, *Das Buch "De Tribus Impostoribus"* (Amsterdam, 1926); *De tribus impostoribus*, ed. G. Bartsch (Berlin, 1960).

CHAPTER 6. *Telesio*

1. Cardano, *De propria vita*, ch. 44 (*Ma vie*, ed. J. Dayre, Paris, 1936, p. 136): "In naturali philosophia sustuli ignem ab elementorum numero."
2. H. Rigault, *Histoire de la Querelle des Anciens et Modernes*, in his *Oeuvres complètes*, Vol. I (Paris, 1859); H. Gillot, *La Querelle des Anciens et des Modernes en France* (Paris, 1914); O. Diede, *Der Streit der Alten und Modernen in der englischen Literaturgeschichte des XVI. und XVII. Jahrhunderts* (Greifswald, 1912); Richard F. Jones, *Ancients and Moderns* (St. Louis, Mo., 1936); G. Margiotta, *Le origini italiane*

174

Notes

de la Querelle des Anciens et des Modernes (Rome, 1953); J. Delvaille, *Essai sur l'histoire de l'idée de progrès jusqu' à la fin du XVIIIe siècle* (Paris, 1910); J. B. Bury, *The Idea of Progress* (London, 1920).

3. Telesio, *De rerum natura,* ed. V. Spampanato, 3 vols. (Modena, 1910–23), I, 1–4.

4. *Ibid.,* I, 5–6.   5. *Ibid.,* II, 93–94.   6. *Ibid.,* I, 105 (Bk. I, ch. 29).

7. For Telesio's concept of space, see E. Cassirer, *Erkenntnisproblem,* I (1911), pp. 258–60; M. Jammer, *Concepts of Space* (New York, 1960), pp. 83–84. These scholars fail to bring out the point that Telesio (Bk. I, chs. 25–28, ed. Spampanato, I, 86–102) repeatedly substitutes "spatium" for the Aristotelian "locus." Thus we have the following phrases: "inane vacuumque spatium" (ed. Spampanato, p. 86); "spatium porro, quod corpore nullo prorsus repletum ac propterea inane vacuumque sit" (*ibid.,* p. 87); "quoniam vero spatium quod antiquioribus nobisque positum est, penitus incorporeum est" (*ibid.,* p. 96). Cf. J. C. Scaliger, *De subtilitate* (Francford, 1592), Bk. V, ch. 3, pp. 15–16: "In suo spatio quod occupat." John Buridan (*Quaestiones super libros IV De caelo et mundo,* Bk. I, qu. 17, ed. E. A. Moody, Cambridge, Mass., 1942, pp. 77–82) raises the question "videtur quod extra caelum sit spatium infinitum," and answers it in the negative.

8. The sequence is place (chs. 1–5), void (chs. 6–9), and time (chs. 10–14).

9. "novorum hominum primum agnoscimus" (*De principiis atque originibus,* in *The Works of Francis Bacon,* ed. J. Spedding, R. L. Ellis, and D. D. Heath, Vol. III, London, 1876, p. 114).

10. See his *Del senso delle cose e della magia* (ed. A. Bruers, Bari, 1925).

11. A letter of Patrizi to Telesio, with Telesio's comments, was published by F. Fiorentino (*Bernardino Telesio,* Vol. II, Florence, 1874, pp. 375–98), evidently from cod. XIV F 43 of the Biblioteca Nazionale in Naples.

CHAPTER 7. *Patrizi*

1. See above, ch. 6, note 11.

2. J. Th. Papademetriou, "The Sources and the Character of *Del Governo de' Regni,*" *Transactions and Proceedings of the American Philological Association,* XCII (1961), 422–39, at pp. 434–35.

3. B. Weinberg, *A History of Literary Criticism in the Italian Renaissance* (Chicago, 1961), I, 600–620; II, 997–1000.

4. Patrizi, *L'Amorosa Filosofia,* ed. John C. Nelson (Florence, 1963); cf. John C. Nelson, "*L'Amorosa Filosofia* di Francesco Patrizi da Cherso," *Rinascimento,* XIII (1962), 89–106.

5. E. Maffei, *I trattati dell'arte storica dal Rinascimento al secolo XVII* (Naples, 1897); Beatrice Reynolds, "Shifting Currents in Historical Criticism," *Journal of the History of Ideas,* XIV (1953), 471–92.

6. Weinberg, II, 765–86; 1024–25. The unpublished sections, preserved in Parma, Biblioteca Palatina, ms. Pal. 408, 417, and 421, are being prepared for a critical edition by Dr. Danilo Aguzzi.

Notes

7. Prof. Harold Cherniss called my attention to the fact that this commentary is not included in the Berlin corpus of Greek commentators on Aristotle (*Commentaria in Aristotelem Graeca*, 23 vols., Berlin, 1882–1907). The Greek text of this unpublished commentary now survives only in one late manuscript (Vienna, Nationalbibliothek, cod. Phil. gr. 189; cf. A. Wartelle, *Inventaire des manuscrits grecs d'Aristote et de ses commentateurs*, Paris, 1963, p. 167, no. 2214). Patrizi's Latin translation, printed in Ferrara in 1583, was based on an older manuscript that Patrizi had sold to Philip II for the Escorial in 1576 (E. Jacobs, "Francesco Patricio und seine Sammlung griechischer Handschriften in der Bibliothek des Escorial," *Zentralblatt fuer Bibliothekswesen*, Vol. XXV, 1908, p. 40, no. 48) and was destroyed by fire in 1671 (R. Beer, "Die Handschriftenschenkung Philipp II. an den Escorial vom Jahre 1576," *Jahrbuch der Kunsthistorischen Sammlungen des Allerhoechsten Kaiserhauses*, Vol. XXIII, Pt. 2, 1903, pp. 43–44). The anonymous commentary in Urbinas graecus 49 of the Vatican Library may be the same work, according to Prof. Cherniss.

8. *De numerorum mysteriis* (1594), to Card. Federico Borromeo, in Milan, Biblioteca Ambrosiana, cod. H 180 inf., f. 142–72.

9. Vatican Library, ms. Barb. gr. 179 and 180.

10. On this text, see Plotinus, *Opera*, ed. P. Henry and H.-R. Schwyzer, Vol. II (Paris and Brussels, 1959), pp. xxvii–xxxi. This work was first translated into Latin by Moses Rovas, revised by Petrus Nicolaus Castellanus, and printed in Rome in 1519. Patrizi reprinted it in the appendix of his *Nova de universis philosophia* (1591) under the title *Mystica Aegyptiorum et Chaldaeorum a Platone voce tradita, ab Aristotele excepta et conscripta philosophia* (*sic*).

11. Several short treatises dealing with Plato and Aristotle are appended to the *Nova de universis philosophia* (1591). On the title page they are referred to as follows: *Capita demum multa in quibus Plato concors, Aristoteles vero Catholicae fidei adversarius ostenditur.*

12. See L. Firpo, "Filosofia italiana e controriforma," *Rivista di Filosofia*, XLI (1950), 150–73, and XLII (1951), 30–47; T. Gregory, "L'Apologia ad Censuram di Francesco Patrizi," *Rinascimento*, IV (1953), 89–104; T. Gregory, "L'Apologia' e le 'Declarationes' di F. Patrizi," in *Medioevo e Rinascimento: Studi in onore di Bruno Nardi* (Florence, 1955), I, 385–424. Manuscripts of Patrizi's defense are in the Vatican Library (ms. Barb. lat. 318) and in Parma (ms. Pal. 665). Another text, entitled *Emendatio*, is preserved in the Archivio dell'Indice and is cited by Firpo (p. 167).

13. See the letter published by A. Solerti, "Autobiografia di Francesco Patricio da Cherso," *Archivio storico per Trieste, l'Istria, e il Trentino*, III (1884–86), 275–81; cf. P. O. Kristeller, *Studies in Renaissance Thought and Letters* (Rome, 1956), p. 290.

14. Cf. Cassirer, *Erkenntnisproblem*, I, 260–67, 398–402.

15. Parma, ms. Pal. 665, and others.

16. I hope some day to study and edit the *Nova de universis philosophia* and the unpublished treatises and letters of Patrizi.

17. *De opificio mundi*, sect. 31.

Notes

18. VI 507e–508c; VII 514a–517c.

19. C. Baeumker, *Witelo* (*Beitraege zur Geschichte der Philosophie des Mittelalters* Vol. III, Pt. 2, Muenster, 1908), pp. 357–425.

20. Ficinus, *De sole et lumine* (*Opera omnia,* I, 965–86, first printed in 1493). The section *De sole* exists in a shorter version dedicated to Eberhard of Wuerttemberg (Stuttgart, ms. HB XV 65, printed Tuebingen, 1547), and the *De lumine* in a shorter version published among the letters (*Opera omnia,* I, 717–20). To the same topic belongs the *Orphica comparatio solis ad Deum* (*ibid.,* pp. 825–26). For the textual questions, see Kristeller, ed., *Supplementum Ficinianum,* I, cxi–cxv, 72–77.

21. Thomas Gianninius, *De lumine et speciebus spiritalibus* . . . (Ferrara, 1615).

22. Kristeller, *Il pensiero,* pp. 102–5 (*The Philosophy,* pp. 106–8).

23. Bk. I. Cf. Lucretius, *De rerum natura,* III, 94–167.

24. Plotinus, *Enneads,* IV, 3, 1–6.

25. Bk. II, f. 66: "Tempus enim post motum vel cum motu est, motus post corpora et cum corporibus."

26. Bk. I, f. 61ᵛ: "Physicorum vero probatissimi dixerunt corpus naturale esse quod constat ex longitudine, latitudine, profunditate et antitypia, quod est resistentia." See Diogenes Laertius, X, 54; *Epicurea,* ed. H. Usener, Leipzig, 1887, fragm. 275, pp. 195–96. Especially important are the passages in Sextus Empiricus (*Adversus mathematicos,* X, 240, 257, and XI, 226), where the term antitypia is repeatedly used.

27. *Enn.,* VI, 1–3.

28. Anaximenes; see H. Diels, *Die Fragmente der Vorsokratiker,* 4th ed. (Berlin, 1922), Vol. I, p. 22, under A5.

29. A. Koyré, *From the Closed World to the Infinite Universe* (New York, 1958), p. 31.

30. Cf. E. Rosen, "Renaissance Science as Seen by Burckhardt and His Successors," in T. Helton, ed., *The Renaissance* (Madison, Wis., 1961), pp. 77–103.

CHAPTER 8. *Bruno*

1. A. Mercati, *Il sommario del processo di Giordano Bruno* (Vatican City, 1942), pp. 55–119; cf. my note in the *Journal of the History of Ideas,* VIII (1947), 240. Out of a large number of charges, only one concerns the plurality of the world (sects. 82–97, pp. 79–83), only one deals with the eternity of the world (sects. 101–9, pp. 84–85), and the motion of the earth is mentioned only as a part of another charge (sect. 256, p. 117).

2. Helga Hajdu, *Das mnemotechnische Schrifttum des Mittelalters* (Vienna, 1936); L. Volkmann, "Ars memorativa," *Jahrbuch der Kunsthistorischen Sammlungen in Wien* (N.S. III, 1929, 111–200); see also Paolo Rossi, *Clavis Universalis: Arti mnemoniche e logica combinatoria da Lullo a Leibniz* (Milan, 1960), and Frances A. Yates, *Giordano Bruno and the Hermetic Tradition* (London and Chicago, 1964).

Notes

3. See the studies by Rossi and Yates.

4. See John C. Nelson, *Renaissance Theory of Love* (New York, 1958).

5. Mercati, sect. 254, p. 114. Here Bruno states that the human soul comes from God and returns to Him.

6. Pt. 1, dialogue 3 (in *Dialoghi morali,* ed. G. Gentile, Bari, 1908, pp. 332–46; *Des fureurs héroïques, e*d. P.-H. Michel, Paris, 1954, pp. 177–99).

7. Dialogue 4 (ed. Gentile, pp. 347–66; ed. Michel, pp. 205–37).

8. *Dialoghi metafisici,* ed. G. Gentile (Bari, 1925), p. 176; translated by S. Greenberg in his *The Infinite in Giordano Bruno* (New York, 1950), p. 109.

9. ed. Gentile, pp. 177–78 (tr. Greenberg, pp. 110–11). Cf. Aristotle, *Metaphysics,* XII 4, 1070 b 22–23.

10. ed. Gentile, p. 179 (tr. Greenberg, p. 111).

11. *Ibid.,* pp. 179–81 (tr. Greenberg, pp. 112–13).

12. *Ibid.,* p. 182 (tr. Greenberg, p. 114).

13. *Ibid.,* pp. 181–94 (tr. Greenberg, pp. 113–22).

14. *Ibid.,* p. 204 (tr. Greenberg, p. 128).

15. *Ibid.,* p. 222 (tr. Greenberg, p. 141).

16. *Ibid.,* p. 223 (tr. Greenberg, p. 142).

17. *Ibid.,* p. 224 (tr. Greenberg, p. 142).

18. *Ibid.,* p. 232 (tr. Greenberg, p. 148).

19. *Ibid.,* p. 239 (tr. Greenberg, p. 153).

20. *Ibid.,* pp. 247–53 (tr. Greenberg, pp. 160–64).

21. *Ibid.,* p. 256 (tr. Greenberg, p. 166).

22. *Ibid.,* p. 254 (tr. Greenberg, p. 165).

23. See above, note 5.

24. A. Koyré, *From the Closed World to the Infinite Universe* (New York, 1958), pp. 35–54.

25. *Ibid.,* p. 33.

26. *Ibid.,* pp. 35–39.

27. *Dialoghi metafisici,* ed. G. Gentile, pp. 288–89; translated by Dorothy W. Singer in her *Giordano Bruno: His Life and Thought* (New York, 1950), pp. 250–51.

28. *Ibid.,* p. 294 (tr. Singer, p. 257).

29. *Ibid.,* p. 298 (tr. Singer, pp. 261–62).

30. *Ibid.,* pp. 338–39 (tr. Singer, p. 302).

31. *Ibid.,* pp. 349–51 (tr. Singer, pp. 311–13).

32. *Ibid.,* pp. 371–79, 406–7 (tr. Singer, pp. 330–39, 366–67).

33. *Ibid.,* p. 373; cf. pp. 349–51, 371–72 (tr. Singer, p. 332; cf. pp. 311–13, 330–31).

34. *Ibid.,* p. 368; cf. p. 340 (tr. Singer, p. 328; cf. pp. 303–4).

35. *Ibid.,* p. 338 (tr. Singer, p. 302).

36. *Ibid.,* pp. 352 and 362; cf. pp. 338–40 (tr. Singer, pp. 314 and 323; cf. pp. 302–4).

37. *Ibid.,* pp. 345–47 (tr. Singer, pp. 308–9).

38. *Ibid.,* pp. 343 and 362 (tr. Singer, pp. 306 and 323).

39. *Ibid.,* pp. 351–52 and 361 (tr. Singer, pp. 313–14 and 322).

Bibliographical
Survey

Bibliographical
Survey

For some bibliography on the general subject of Renaissance philosophy, see F. Ueberweg, *Grundriss der Geschichte der Philosophie,* Vol. III, 12th ed. (by M. Frischeisen-Koehler and W. Moog), Berlin, 1924; P. O. Kristeller and J. H. Randall, Jr., "The Study of the Philosophies of the Renaissance," *Journal of the History of Ideas,* II (1941), 449–96; T. Helton, ed., *The Renaissance* (Madison, Wis., 1961 and 1964). Of the general works on the Renaissance, J. Burckhardt's *Civilization of the Renaissance in Italy* (many editions) contains much on humanism but little on the other philosophical currents, whereas J. A. Symonds's *Renaissance in Italy* (many editions) discusses the subject more fully but is largely outdated. Of the general histories of philosophy, G. De Ruggero, *Storia della filosofia* (several editions), F. Copleston, *A History of Philosophy,* Vol. III, "Ockham to Suarez" (Westminster, Md., 1953), and especially John H. Randall, Jr., *The Career of Philosophy* (New York, 1962), contain an ample account of Renaissance thought. A. A. Maurer, *Medieval Philosophy* (New York, 1962), contains a full treatment of Ficino and Pomponazzi. For a systematic treatment of Italian Renaissance thought, see E. Garin, *La filosofia,* 2 vols. (Milan, 1947), and *L'umanesimo italiano* (Bari, 1952); G. Saitta, *Il pensiero italiano nell' umanesimo e nel Rinascimento,* 3 vols. (Bologna, 1949–51).

The following works are less complete or systematically arranged, but cover important aspects of the subject: F. Fiorentino, *Il risorgimento filosofico del Quattrocento* (Naples, 1885); W. Dilthey, "Auffassung und Analyse des Menschen im 15. und 16. Jahrhundert" (first published 1890–92), in his *Gesammelte Schriften,* Vol. II (Leipzig and Berlin, 1914), pp. 1–89; G. Gentile, *La filosofia* (Milan, 1904–15), revised under the title *Storia della filosofia italiana,* in his *Opere complete* (Florence, 1961); G. Gentile, *Studi sul Rinascimento,* 2d ed. (Florence, 1936); G. Gentile, *Il pensiero italiano del Rinascimento,* 3d ed. (Florence, 1940); E. Cassirer, *Das Erkenntnisproblem,* Vol. I, 2d ed. (Berlin, 1911); E. Cassirer, *Individuum und Kosmos in der Philosophie der Renaissance* (Leipzig and Berlin, 1927, reprinted Darmstadt, 1962), translated by M. Domandi under the title *The Individual and the Cosmos in Renaissance Philosophy* (New York, 1963); G. Toffanin, *Storia dell'umanesimo,* 3 vols. (Bologna, 1950); P. O. Kristeller, *Studies in Renaissance Thought and Letters* (Rome, 1956); P. O. Kristeller, *Renaissance Thought* (New York, 1961); E. Garin, *La cultura filosofica del Rinascimento italiano* (Florence, 1961).

Collections of texts: E. Garin, ed., *Prosatori latini del Quattrocento* (Milan, 1952), in Latin and Italian; E. Cassirer, P. O. Kristeller, and J. H. Randall, Jr., eds., *The Renaissance Philosophy of Man* (Chicago, 1948), in English.

For important related aspects of Renaissance thought and learning, see G. Voigt, *Die Wiederbelebung des classischen Alterthums,* 3d ed., 2 vols. (Berlin, 1893); R. Sabbadini, *Le scoperte dei codici latini e greci ne' secoli XIV e XV,* 2 vols. (Florence, 1905–14); J. E. Sandys, *A History of Classical Scholarship,* Vol. II (Cambridge, 1908); L. Thorndike, *A History of Magic and Experimental Science,* 8 vols. (New York, 1923–58); L. Thorndike, *Science and Thought in the Fifteenth Century* (New York, 1929); D. P. Walker, *Spiritual and Demonic Magic from Ficino to Campanella* (London, 1958); Paolo Rossi, *Clavis Universalis: Arti mnemoniche e logica combinatoria da Lullo a Leibniz* (Milan, 1960); E. von Aster, *Raum und Zeit in der Geschichte der Philosophie und Physik* (Munich, 1922); Max Jammer, *Concepts of Space* (Cambridge, Mass., 1954, and New York, 1960); A. Koyré, *From the Closed World to the Infinite Universe* (New York, 1958).

CHAPTER I. *Petrarch*

For a bibliography of recent studies on humanism, see P. O. Kristeller, "Studies on Renaissance Humanism During the Last Twenty Years," *Studies in the Renaissance,* IX (1962), 7–30; C. Trinkaus, art., "Humanism," *Encyclopedia of World Art,* Vol. VII (New York, 1963), cols. 701–43. See especially C. Trinkaus, *Adversity's Noblemen* (New York, 1940); W. Rüegg, *Cicero und der Humanismus* (Zurich, 1946); H. Baron, *The Crisis of the Early Italian Renaissance,* 2 vols. (Princeton, N.J., 1955); B. L. Ullman, *Studies in the Italian Renaissance* (Rome, 1955); T. E. Mommsen, *Medieval and Renaissance Studies,* ed. E. F. Rice (Ithaca, N.Y., 1959).

Editions of Petrarch texts: Of the Edizione Nazionale, only certain volumes have appeared, notably *Le Familiari,* ed. V. Rossi and U. Bosco, 4 vols. (Florence, 1933–42), and *Rerum Memorandarum Libri,* ed. G. Billanovich (Florence, 1943). For other texts, see the important collection of Petrarch's *Prose,* ed.

G. Martellotti *et al.* (Milan and Naples, 1955); *Le traité De sui ipsius et multo-rum ignorantia,* ed. L. M. Capelli (Paris, 1906); R. Weiss, *Un inedito Petrar-chesco* (Rome, 1950). For other Latin writings, the *Opera* (Basel, 1581) must still be used. Petrarch's *Secret* was translated into English by W. H. Draper (London, 1911), and his *De ignorantia,* with excellent notes, by H. Nachod (in E. Cassirer *et al.,* eds., *The Renaissance Philosophy of Man,* Chicago, 1948, pp. 47–133), who added the letter on the ascent of Mont Ventoux (pp. 36–46) and some other letters.

For Petrarch's life and works, see Edward H. R. Tatham, *Francesco Petrarca,* 2 vols. (London, 1925–26); U. Bosco, *Petrarca* (Turin, 1946); numerous studies by Ernest H. Wilkins, especially *Studies in the Life and Works of Petrarch* (Cambridge, Mass., 1955) and *Life of Petrarch* (Chicago, 1961); M. Bishop, *Petrarch and His World* (Bloomington, Ind., 1963). For Petrarch's culture, see P. De Nolhac, *Pétrarque et l'humanisme,* 2 vols., 2d ed. (Paris, 1907); P. De Nolhac, "De patrum et medii aevi scriptorum codicibus in bibliotheca Petrarcae olim collectis," *Revue des Bibliothèques,* II (1892), 241–79; G. Billanovich, *Petrarca letterato, vol. 1: Lo scrittoio del Petrarca* (Rome, 1947). For specific aspects of Petrarch's thought, see P. P. Gerosa, *L'umanesimo agostiniano del Petrarca* (Turin, 1927); Elena Razzoli, *Agostinismo e religiosità del Petrarca* (Milan, 1937); K. Heitmann, *Fortuna und Virtus: Eine Studie zu Petrarcas Lebensweisheit* (Cologne and Graz, 1958). See also J. H. Whitfield, *Petrarch and the Renascence* (Oxford, 1943). For further literature on Petrarch, and especially on his poetry, see N. Sapegno, *Il Trecento,* 5th ed. (Milan, 1948).

CHAPTER 2. *Valla*

Editions of texts: *Opera omnia* (Basel, 1540), reprinted with substantial additions (2 vols., Turin, 1962); *De libero arbitrio,* ed. Maria Anfossi (Florence, 1934). A critical edition of the *Dialectica* is being prepared by G. Zippel, and one of the *De voluptate* by Maristella Lorch. For Italian translations of *De volup-tate* and *De libero arbitrio,* see *Scritti filosofici e religiosi,* ed. G. Radetti (Florence, 1953). The text and an Italian translation of the *De libero arbitrio* are also to be found in Garin's *Prosatori latini del Quattrocento,* pp. 523–93. For an English translation, see Christopher B. Coleman, *The Treatise of Lorenzo Valla on the Donation of Constantine* (New Haven, 1922). An English translation of the *De libero arbitrio,* with notes, by Charles Trinkaus, is in E. Cassirer *et al.,* eds., *The Renaissance Philosophy of Man,* pp. 155–82.

For Valla's life and works, see Girolamo Mancini, *Vita di Lorenzo Valla* (Florence, 1891); L. Barozzi and R. Sabbadini, *Studi sul Panormita e sul Valla* (Florence, 1891); Franco Gaeta, *Lorenzo Valla* (Naples, 1955).

CHAPTER 3. *Ficino*

For Renaissance Platonism, in addition to the works cited in the general bibliography, see Nesca A. Robb, *Neoplatonism of the Italian Renaissance* (London, 1935); R. Klibansky, *The Continuity of the Platonic Tradition During the Middle Ages* (London, 1939 and 1950); John C. Nelson, *Renaissance Theory of Love* (New York, 1958).

Editions of texts: *Opera omnia*, 2 vols. (Basel, 1576, and Turin, 1959); P. O. Kristeller, ed., *Supplementum Ficinianum,* 2 vols. (Florence, 1937); P. O. Kristeller, *Studies* (1956), pp. 55–97, 146–50; Ficino, *Commentaire sur le Banquet de Platon,* ed. R. Marcel (Paris, 1956); Sears Jayne, *John Colet and Marsilio Ficino* (London, 1963). For English translations, see Marsilio Ficino, *Commentary on Plato's Symposium,* ed. and tr. Sears Jayne (*University of Missouri Studies,* Vol. XIX, No. 1, Columbia, 1944); "Five Questions Concerning the Mind," tr. Josephine Burroughs, in E. Cassirer *et al.,* eds., *The Renaissance Philosophy of Man,* pp. 193–212.

For Ficino's life, works, and influence, see A. Della Torre, *Storia dell'Accademia Platonica di Firenze* (Florence, 1902); A. M. J. Festugière, *La philosophie de l'amour de Marsile Ficin et son influence sur la littérature française au XVIe siècle* (Paris, 1941); R. Marcel, *Marsile Ficin* (Paris, 1958). For his thought, see G. Saitta, *Marsilio Ficino e la filosofia dell'umanesimo,* 3d ed. (Bologna, 1954); P. O. Kristeller, *The Philosophy of Marsilio Ficino,* tr. Virginia Conant (New York, 1943); P. O. Kristeller, *Il pensiero filosofico di Marsilio Ficino* (Florence, 1953), the same work revised and more fully documented; A. Chastel, *Marsile Ficin et l'art* (Paris, 1954); M. Schiavone, *Problemi filosofici in Marsilio Ficino* (Milan, 1957).

CHAPTER 4. *Pico*

Editions of texts: *De hominis dignitate, Heptaplus, De ente et uno, e Scritti vari,* ed. E. Garin (Florence, 1942); *Disputationes adversus astrologiam divinatricem,* ed. Garin, 2 vols. (Florence, 1946–52); *Opera* (Basel, 1572). For English translations, see Pico, *His Life by His Nephew Giovanni Francesco Pico* (and other writings), tr. Sir Thomas More, ed. J. M. Rigg (London, 1890); *A Pla-*

tonick Discourse upon Love, tr. Thomas Stanley (1651), ed. E. G. Gardner (Boston, 1914); *Of Being and Unity,* tr. V. M. Hamm (Milwaukee, 1943). The *Oration* is available in three translations: *The Very Elegant Speech on the Dignity of Man,* tr. Charles G. Wallis (Annapolis, Md., 1940); *Oration on the Dignity of Man,* tr. Elizabeth L. Forbes (in E. Cassirer *et al.,* eds., *The Renaissance Philosophy of Man,* Chicago, 1948, pp. 223–54, reprinted with the Latin text in *Oratio de hominis dignitate,* Lexington, Ky., 1953); *Oration on the Dignity of Man,* tr. A. Robert Caponigri (Chicago, 1956).

Of the numerous studies on Pico, the following are especially important: E. Anagnine, *G. Pico della Mirandola* (Bari, 1937); E. Garin, *Giovanni Pico della Mirandola* (Florence, 1937); E. Garin, *La cultura filosofica del Rinascimento italiano* (Florence, 1961); E. Garin, *Giovanni Pico della Mirandola* (Mirandola, 1963); L. Dorez and L. Thuasne, *Pic de la Mirandole en France* (Paris, 1897); P. Kibre, *The Library of Pico della Mirandola* (New York, 1936); Avery Dulles, *Princeps Concordiae: Pico della Mirandola and the Scholastic Tradition* (Cambridge, Mass., 1941); E. Cassirer, "Giovanni Pico della Mirandola," *Journal of the History of Ideas,* III (1942), 123–44; 319–46; E. Monnerjahn, *Giovanni Pico della Mirandola* (Wiesbaden, 1960). The proceedings of the Pico Congress held in 1963 will be published in the near future.

CHAPTER 5. *Pomponazzi*

For Renaissance Aristotelianism, see E. Renan, *Averroès et l'averroïsme,* 2d ed. (Paris, 1861) and many editions; B. Nardi, *Sigieri di Brabante nel pensiero del Rinascimento italiano* (Rome, 1945); B. Nardi, *Saggi sull'aristotelismo padovano dal secolo XIV al XVI* (Florence, 1958); J. H. Randall, Jr., *The School of Padua and the Emergence of Modern Science* (Padua, 1961); P. O. Kristeller, *La tradizione aristotelica nel Rinascimento* (Padua, 1962).

Editions of texts: *De immortalitate animae,* ed. G. Gentile (Messina, 1925), ed. G. Morra (Bologna, 1954); *De fato,* ed. R. Lemay (Lugano, 1957); *De naturalium effectuum causis sive de incantationibus* (Basel, 1556, and in *Opera,* Basel, 1567); *Tractatus acutissimi* (Venice, 1525); P. O. Kristeller, "Two Unpublished Questions on the Soul by Pietro Pomponazzi," *Medievalia et Humanistica,* IX (1955), 76–101, and X (1956), 151. An English translation of the *De immortalitate animae* by W. H. Hay was first published, with a facsimile of the early edition, in Haverford in 1938, and later in E. Cassirer *et al.,* eds., *The Renaissance Philosophy of Man* (Chicago, 1948), pp. 280–381.

For his thought, see F. Fiorentino, *Pietro Pomponazzi* (Florence, 1868); Andrew H. Douglas, *The Philosophy and Psychology of Pietro Pomponazzi* (Cambridge, 1910). See also a series of articles by B. Nardi in the *Giornale Critico della Filosofia Italiana,* Vols. XXIX–XXXV (1950–56); Don Cameron Allen, *Doubt's Boundless Sea: Skepticism and Faith in the Renaissance* (Baltimore, 1964), pp. 29–45; D. A. Jorio, "The Problem of the Soul and the Unity of Man in Pietro Pomponazzi," The New Scholasticism, XXXVII (1963), 293–311.

CHAPTER 6. *Telesio*

For the philosophers of nature, see the studies by Cassirer and Koyré in the general bibliography.

Editions of texts: *De rerum natura,* ed. V. Spampanato, 3 vols. (Modena, 1910–23).

For studies of Telesio, see F. Fiorentino, *Bernardino Telesio,* 2 vols. (Florence, 1872–74); Neil C. Van Deusen, *Telesio: The First of the Moderns* (thesis, Columbia University, New York, 1932); N. Abbagnano, *Bernardino Telesio* (Milan, 1941); G. Soleri, *Telesio* (Brescia, 1945).

CHAPTER 7. *Patrizi*

For Patrizi bibliography, see Brickman below; Lega Nazionale di Trieste, *Onoranze a Francesco Patrizi da Cherso, Catalogo della Mostra Bibliografica* (Trieste, 1957).

Editions of texts: *Discussiones peripateticae* (Basel, 1581); *Nova de universis philosophia* (Ferrara, 1591, and Venice, 1593); *L'Amorosa Filosofia,* ed. John C. Nelson (Florence, 1963); an edition of the *Poetica,* including its unpublished sections, is being prepared by Dr. Danilo Aguzzi.

For Patrizi's life and difficulties with the Congregation of the Index, see A. Solerti, "Autobiografia di Francesco Patricio da Cherso," *Archivio storico per Trieste, l'Istria e il Trentino,* III (1884–86), 275–81; L. Firpo, "Filosofia italiana e controriforma," *Rivista di Filosofia,* XLI (1950), 150–73, and XLII (1951), 30–47; T. Gregory, "L'Apologia ad Censuram di Francesco Patrizi," *Rinascimento,* IV (1953), 89–104; T. Gregory, "L''Apologia' e le 'Declarationes' di F. Patrizi," in *Medioevo e Rinascimento: Studi in onore di Bruno Nardi* (Florence, 1955), I, 385–424.

For his thought, see Paola Maria Arcari, *Il pensiero politico di Francesco Patrizi da Cherso* (Rome, 1935); Benjamin Brickman, *An Introduction to Francesco Patrizi's Nova de universis philosophia* (thesis, Columbia University, New

Bibliographical Survey

York, 1941, with bibliography). See also E. Jacobs, "Francesco Patrizi und seine Sammlung griechischer Handschriften in der Bibliothek des Escorial," *Zentralblatt fuer Bibliothekswesen*, XXV (1908), 19–47; J. Th. Papademetriou, "The Sources and the Character of *Del Governo de' Regni*," *Transactions and Proceedings of the American Philological Association*, XCII (1961), 422–39 (esp. 434–35); John C. Nelson, "L'"Amorosa Filosofia' di Francesco Patrizi da Cherso," *Rinascimento*, XIII (1962), 89–106.

CHAPTER 8. *Bruno*

For Bruno bibliography, see V. Salvestrini, *Bibliografia delle opere di Giordano Bruno* (Pisa, 1926, revised edition by L. Firpo, Florence, 1958).

Editions of texts: *Opere italiane*, 2d ed., 3 vols., ed. V. Spampanato and G. Gentile (Bari, 1923–27); *Dialoghi italiani*, 3d ed., ed. G. Aquilecchia (Florence, 1958); *Opera latine conscripta*, ed. F. Fiorentino *et al.*, 3 vols. in 6 (Naples, 1879–91, and Stuttgart, 1962); *Des fureurs héroïques*, ed. P.-H. Michel (Paris, 1954); *Due dialoghi sconosciuti e due dialoghi noti*, ed. G. Aquilecchia (Rome, 1957); for a new text to be published soon, see G. Aquilecchia, "Lezioni inedite di Giordano Bruno in un codice della Biblioteca universitaria di Jena," Accademia Nazionale dei Lincei, *Rendiconti della Classe di Scienze Morali, Storiche e Filologiche,* Ser. 8, Vol. XVII (1962), pp. 463–85. For English translations, see "Concerning the Cause, Principle and One," in S. Greenberg (see below); "On the Infinite Universe and Worlds," in D. Singer (see below); *The Heroic Enthusiasts*, tr. L. Williams, 2 vols. (London, 1887–89); *The Heroic Frenzies*, tr. Paul E. Memmo (thesis, Columbia University, New York, in microfilm, Ann Arbor, 1959); *Cause, Principle and Unity*, tr. Jack Lindsay (Castle Hedingham, Essex, 1962, and New York, 1964).

For Bruno's life and trial, see V. Spampanato, *Vita di Giordano Bruno*, 2 vols. (Messina, 1921); *Documenti della vita di Giordano Bruno*, ed. V. Spampanato (Florence, 1934); A. Mercati, *Il sommario del processo di Giordano Bruno* (Vatican City, 1942); L. Firpo, "Il processo di Giordano Bruno," *Rivista storica italiana*, LX (1948), 542–97, and LXI (1949), 5–59.

For his thought, see F. Tocco, *Le opere latine di Giordano Bruno* (Florence, 1889); L. Olschki, *Giordano Bruno* (Bari, 1927); Sidney Greenberg, *The Infinite in Giordano Bruno* (New York, 1950); Dorothy W. Singer, *Giordano Bruno: His Life and Thought* (New York, 1950); Irving L. Horowitz, *The Renaissance Philosophy of Giordano Bruno* (New York, 1952)—I disagree with many views of this author; John C. Nelson, *Renaissance Theory of Love* (New

York, 1958); P.-H. Michel, *La cosmologie de Giordano Bruno* (Paris, 1962); Frances A. Yates, *Giordano Bruno and the Hermetic Tradition* (London and Chicago, 1964).

Appendix

For this section, I may be permitted to refer to some of my other studies: "Humanism and Scholasticism in the Italian Renaissance," last printed in my *Renaissance Thought* (New York, 1961), pp. 92–119, 153–66; "Umanesimo italiano e Bisanzio," *Lettere Italiane*, XVI (1964), 1–14; and my forthcoming Wimmer lecture, *Renaissance Philosophy and the Mediaeval Tradition*. For the contribution of the humanists to classical scholarship, see the works by Voigt, Sabbadini, and Sandys cited in the general section; for their contribution to literature, see V. Rossi, *Il Quattrocento*, 4th ed. (Milan, 1949); for the contribution of the humanists to ethics, see P. O. Kristeller, "The Moral Thought of Renaissance Humanism," in *Chapters in Western Civilization* (Columbia University, New York, Vol. I, 3d ed., 1961), pp. 289–335. For the origin of the terms *humanista* and *studia humanitatis,* see also A. Campana, "The Origin of the Word 'Humanist,' " *Journal of the Warburg and Courtauld Institutes,* IX (1946), 60–73.

For the Latin translations from the Greek, see J. T. Muckle, "Greek Works Translated Directly into Latin Before 1350," *Mediaeval Studies,* IV (1942), 33–42, and V (1943), 102–14; *Corpus Platonicum Medii Aevi,* ed. R. Klibansky; *Aristoteles Latinus,* ed. G. Lacombe *et al.,* 3 vols. (Vol. I, Rome, 1939, Vol. II, Cambridge, 1955, and Vol. III, Bruges and Paris, 1961).

For Renaissance rhetoric and poetics and their medieval background, see C. S. Baldwin, *Medieval Rhetoric and Poetic* (New York, 1928), and *Renaissance Literary Theory and Practice* (New York, 1939); Donald L. Clark, *Rhetoric and Poetry in the Renaissance* (New York, 1922); A. Buck, *Italienische Dichtungslehren vom Mittelalter bis zum Ausgang der Renaissance* (Tuebingen, 1952).

For Greek studies prior to the humanistic period, see several studies by R. Weiss, especially "The Greek Culture of South Italy in the Later Middle Ages," *Proceedings of the British Academy,* XXXVII (1951), 23–50; K. M. Setton, "The Byzantine Background to the Italian Renaissance," *Proceedings of the American Philosophical Society,* C (1956), 1–76.

Index

Index

Index

Index

Lipsius, Justus, 36
Locke, John, 107
Lucretius, 39, 103, 122, 131, 136
Lullian art, 130
Luther, Martin, 78, 92
Lyons, poets of, 51

Malebranche, Nicolas de, 52
Manetti, Giannozzo, 16, 66
Marguerite of Navarre, 51
Mazzoni, Jacopo, 114, 117
Medici, Cosimo de', 39f
Medici, Lorenzo de', 50, 57
Medici, Piero de', 57
Medigo, Elia del, 56
Melanchthon, Philip, 10, 56
Mocenigo, Giovanni, 128
Montaigne, Michel de, 13, 36, 67
More, Thomas, 12, 51, 92
Mussato, Albertino, 162

Nature, philosophers of, 95f, 110–13, 122, 142
Neoplatonism, 38, 60, 64f, 69, 120f, 137; see also Ficino, Plotinus
Newton, Isaac, 103–8 passim
Nizolius, Marius, 35

Orpheus, 23, 38, 59

Paracelsus, Theophrastus, 51, 96
Parmenides, 53
Patrizi, Francesco: and Telesio, 107, 110–11, 112; life, 113; writings, 113–15; rejects Aristotle, 114f, 117; on mathematics, 115–16, 117, 123–24; as Platonist, 115ff, 123; on light, 119–20; cosmology, 121–25
Paul, St., 29, 47, 61
Petrarca, Francesco: life, 5; influence, 5–6, 10f, 17–18, 48; rejects scholasticism, 6,

8, 11f; and classical learning, 7–10; temperament, 7, 13ff; and Christianity, 11–12, 16–17; on man, 15f; mentioned, 37, 58, 114, 152, 162f
Philip II of Spain, 113
Philo of Alexandria, 118
Philoponus, John, 115
Pico, Gianfrancesco, 64
Pico della Mirandola, Giovanni: on man, 16, 66–68, 70–71, life of, 54–57; and Platonism, 54–55; and Aristotle, 55, 63–64; and Ficino, 55, 60, 69; writings, 57–58; defends scholastic philosophy, 58f; syncretism, 59–62, 69; on Cabalism, 61–62; and religion, 68–69; influence of, 68ff, 75
Pio, Alberto, 76
Plato, 10, 23, 28, 38–45 passim, 52, 59, 61–65 passim, 69, 75
Platonic Academy of Florence, 10, 37–42 passim, 48, 51, 54–55, 57
Platonic love, 45, 47–48
Platonism, Renaissance, 11, 37f, 45, 117, 141–42; see also Neoplatonism
Pléiade, 51
Plethon, Gemistos, 39
Plotinus, 39, 42f, 45, 52, 63f, 120, 122, 131, 135
Plutarch, 75
Poggio Bracciolini, 7
Poliziano, Angelo, 56f
Pomponazzi, Pietro: on magic, 68; on immortality of soul, 75f, 78–81, 84–85, 88f; life of, 76, 86; and Stoics, 76, 83; on Aristotle, 77, 82; on fate, 78; on intellect, 79–80, 82; on virtue, 82–83; and Ficino, 75, 86–87; influence of, 88–90
Pontano, Gioviano, 68
Proclus Diadochus, 115
Pythagoras, 23, 38, 53, 59

Quintilian, 34

Index

Ramus, Peter, 35, 51
Reformation, 91–94
Renan, Ernest, 89
Reuchlin, Johann, 51, 62
Ruscelli, Girolamo, 113

Salutati, Coluccio, 65, 150, 163
Savonarola, Girolamo, 57, 69
Scholastic philosophy, 17, 27, 34, 58f
Scholasticism, definition of, 6
Seneca, 8, 16, 22, 37
Servetus, Michael, 92
Sextus Empiricus, 23
Sidney, Sir Philip, 128
Soul: pleasures of, 28, 31; immortality of, 39, 45–47, 76, 78–81, 84–89; intermediate position of, 43, 66, 122; ascends toward God, 44, 46, 131; twofold nature of, 99–106; world soul, 122, 132f
Spinoza, Baruch, 52, 84, 138
Steuchus, Augustinus, 50, 172
Stoicism, Stoics, 8, 23, 27, 29ff, 65, 78, 83, 105
Syncretism, philosophical, 59–62, 69

Tasso, Torquato, 114
Telesio, Antonio, 97
Telesio, Bernardino; life of, 97; on space, 98, 103–5, 124, 175; criticizes Aristotle, 98f, 102f; doctrine of two souls, 99–106; on knowledge, 100–106 *passim*; influence of, 105, 106–9, 123; compared with Patrizi, 110–12
Thomas Aquinas, St., 12, 39f, 59, 79ff, 148, 159
Truth, double, theory of, 7, 84, 86

Universities, emergence of, 73f

Valla, Lorenzo: life, 24; influence of, 25, 34–35; rejects scholastic philosophy, 27, 34f; *On Free Will*, 25–27; *On Pleasure*, 27–32; on Stoics, 31; criticizes Aristotle, 32, 34; religious beliefs, 31, 33; *Dialectical Disputations*, 33–34
Vanini, Giulio Cesare, 88
Verino, Francesco, il Secondo, 117
Vico, Giambattista, 97
Virgilio, Giovanni del, 162
Vittorino da Feltre, 19
Vives, Juan Luis, 6, 36, 150

Will and intellect, 17, 40, 44

Zabarella, Jacopo, 10
Zoroaster, 23, 38, 50, 53, 59ff, 69, 115f